Swinging From the Chandeliers

SOPHIA SMITH

New York
©2019

This is a work of fiction. Names, characters, places, and incidents either are the product of the author's imagination or are used fictitiously. Any resemblance to actual persons, living or dead, events, or locales is entirely coincidental.

To Chloe and Alexander, I love you more than life.
You are amazing, and magical and brilliant.

Photo credit front cover: Maurizio Bacci for Studio Babaldi
Copyright © 2019 Sophia Smith

Table of Contents

1. Looking for Mr. Agnelli
2. Betty and the Fur Coat
3. I Want to Marry Sting
4. Prada Shoes
5. Salinger and Lebowitz
6. The Cowboy of Madison Avenue
7. I Lost My Underwear at Château Marmont
8. Tree Killer
9. A Pro Tried to Kill Me at Hotel Costes
10. 'Twas the Night Before Thanksgiving
11. Running Away From Home Across the Street
12. Pine Forest
13. I Left My Teeth in Sarasota
14. The Sophia Questionnaire

Looking for Mr. Agnelli

I was sitting by the pool at the Hotel Cipriani in Venice. Something I had dreamed of my whole life. I was waiting to see a bevy of supermodels, rock stars, European royalty, and the glittering jet set . Most of the guests were just lounging by the side of the pool, nary dipping their toes into the beautiful aqua vessel laid out before them.

I was wearing a new navy blue and white striped bikini and trying to look as cool and nonplussed as possible. I was trying to scope out the crowd at the pool, without looking like I cared. Soon, out of the corner of my eye, I saw the person I had hoped and dreamed I would see, but never expected to actually lay my eyes on.

Laying on the lounge about thirty feet to my left was Mr. Gianni Agnelli. The chairman of the Fiat corporation himself. Of course I expected him to be accompanied by a beautiful, elegant woman, however, he had about four gorgeous women surrounding him. Doting on him, fawning over him and practically fainting over him.

"Oh, Gianni."

"Yes, Gianni."

"More champagne, Gianni?"

"Do you need some suntan oil Gianni?" as one of the brunette beauties rubbed the oil over his arms and chest.

I was reading Truman Capote's book, *Music For Chameleons*, but I was actually unable to concentrate and was much more interested in Mr. Agnelli, his entourage and what was happening around the pool. Certainly everyone at the hotel was staring at him. All the men wishing they were him, and all the women wishing they were his companion.

He received a phone call, so he was beckoned to the poolside cabana bar where he took the seemingly extremely important call. He runs The Fiat Corporation after all, and running Fiat is like running Italy itself. As he slowly but carefully walked back to his spot by the pool, he scanned his audience. Shaking a few hands and stopping to kiss a few ladies hello.

To my surprise, he stopped at the end of my lounge.

"Are you American?" Gianni inquired.

"Yes, and I love Italy! It is the most beautiful, exciting and wonderful place I have ever visited," I replied.

He said, "I am Gianni Agnelli, it is a pleasure to make your acquaintance, I'm going to have lunch at my table now if you would like to join me and my friends, I would be honored."

Little old me? From Lewiston, New York? Getting invited to dine with Mr. Gianni Agnelli and become a part of the jet set? For even an afternoon? My heart was pounding and one million butterflies were scrambling around my stomach - all the while I was trying to suck in my stomach and make it look as flat as possible while I tried to exude an air of athleticism and nonchalance, instead of the look the European women were going for poolside. By this I mean long false eyelashes, teased hair, frosted lipstick and little high heeled slippers while they were sitting at the pool in the hot, hot sun trying to look like they were not melting.

I said, " I would love to join you Mr. Agnelli, but I'm taking a dip in the pool first!"

With that, I took off my sunglasses, walked to the deep end of the gigantic pool - which happens to be the largest swimming pool in Europe - but more on that later.

I dove into the crisp and chilly water.

Gianni loved this! "Finally someone is making good use of this pool except only me!" he said with a movie star smile.

He dove into the water with his sunglasses and gold jewelry on and didn't seem to care about messing up his perfectly coiffed hair or getting his extremely expensive tortoise shell sunglasses covered in chlorinated water.

We had lunch at The Grill, the most historic and fashionable restaurant at the Cipriani. They have another fine dining restaurant, but that is not suitable for pool attire. Presidents and prime ministers, movie stars and aristocrats have all dined here since Hotel Cipriani opened.

Gianni introduced me to everyone at his table. There was the French Ambassador, Princess Caroline of Monaco, Carlo Ciampi, who later became the president of Italy, Henry Kissinger, and the women from the pool of course.

After lunch he said to his captain, "Get the boat ready we are going for a cruise."

He gestured for me to join their group so I wasn't about to second guess any of this great fun and luck and luxury that was being thrown my way. We sped off in his Italian cigarette boat that had a Fiat engine, what else?

Rumor had it that it was actually a Ferrari engine but I didn't ask any questions. I was a guest and he was the host with the most. We sped away from the island of Giudecca with all eyes on us.

We cruised around the Adriatic for the rest of the afternoon watching the sun sparkle on the Piazza San Marco, Palazzo Ducale, Hotel Danieli, and the rest of the gorgeous legendary buildings on the Canale di San Marco.

Soon Gianni motioned for the captain to leave the driver's seat, and he took over. What fun! Gianni threw caution to the wind, and drove the boat with absolutely no concern for anything in his path. Fishing boats, yachts, sailboats and swimmers and anyone else you can think of knew they had better get out of Gianni's way in a hurry! When we all finally returned to the hotel, I was sun-drenched and waterlogged, exhausted yet exhilarated.

I said, "Thank you so much Mr. Agnelli, it was the best afternoon of my life!"

Gianni replied, "Well, certainly Sophia you are joining us for dinner!"

I went back to my room showered and changed and put on my most glamorous dress as quickly as possible. I went down to the bar and nobody was there yet. It was around 7 o'clock. I was told Mr. Agnelli and his party dine anywhere from 9 o'clock until midnight and they keep the kitchen open for him no matter when he deigns to arrive.

I sat at the bar and nursed my Bellini because the drinks were very expensive. After all I was putting the drink on my own hotel room bill, not Mr. Agnelli's.

When Gianni finally walked through the door of the dining room, it was as if Jesus Christ himself walked in. Surrounded by his faithful disciples, male and female, all vying for a little piece of his time and attention.

He walked over to the bar kissed my hand and said "I hope I have not kept you waiting too long. Come to my table."

Gianni pulled out the chair next to his for me, and I sat down. All of the entourage from the afternoon boat ride was there, plus a few new women and a German businessman. Gianni was the ultimate gentleman and host, introducing everyone, kissing all the ladies, and holding court like none other. He was telling jokes in English, then Italian, then German for the group's pleasure. He regaled us with his stories of meeting and making love to Marilyn Monroe, Grace Kelly, and Jackie Kennedy. He said he could tell us which was his favorite, but that wouldn't be very Italian of him.

We started out with Bellinis, moved along to French champagne , then to some scrumptious Italian red wine which tasted like velvet and like nothing I had ever tasted before. The waiters came to our table like a regiment of soldiers, laying down all of our plates at the same time. It was like a symphony of great service, amazing food and the best wine you have ever tasted!
At the end of the evening Gianni told everybody thank you for coming and that he would see them tomorrow.

Then he looked at me and said, "Please stay."

He asked me if I wanted to go for a walk along the canal in the moonlight. Of course I said yes.

We walked along the canals of the Adriatic with the glorious full moon shining above us, illuminating the ancient churches, homes, gardens, docked vaporettos and gondolas. All was tranquil and still, we could hear the waves gently lapping on the now quiet hub of tourists and titans.

He gently took my hand as we were strolling, which for Gianni was nothing, however, to me it escalated the butterflies in my stomach into a churning tango of nerves and anticipation. Gianni was a master of the universe, a king of business, a champion diplomat and a complete professional seducer of women.

Gianni remarked that the moonlight shining on my face made me look like "an angel walking on earth" as he wrapped his arm around my shoulder and turned my lips to meet his - a move he no doubt perfected many decades ago. We kissed with passion, with emotion and with feeling. Gianni couldn't stop complimenting my beauty, my wit, my long hair, my charm; he really knew what to say to a woman to make her feel like a goddess.

We strolled back to Hotel Cipriani, and we kissed on the terrace of the hotel for what seemed like a lifetime. He lifted up my chin and looked into my eyes deeply and said, "There is nothing I would enjoy more than to make love to you tonight."

I was excited, scared, and also pretty nervous. I knew I didn't want to be an easy conquest for Gianni, who had the pick of the litter of the most beautiful women in the world.

I suggested one more nightcap at the bar without saying yes or no to his proposition. If I leapt into bed with him, would he consider me just one more in the crowd of his stable? If I played hard to get, would he respect me more - and find me more alluring because I didn't jump at the chance to be with him?

The scene was delightful as we sat outside at the bar, the moonlight was twinkling on the ethereal swimming pool, a trio was playing samba music in the corner. Once again, all the waiters and hotel guests (who were still awake at this ungodly hour) were bowing to Gianni like royalty and treating him like an HRH. I was enjoying every minute of his attention, and the gentle caresses he was cascading me with. As we were sipping our martinis, he had his hand on my knees, my legs, my hair or around my arm and all the patrons of the hotel were staring.

Gianni looked into my eyes again and said, "I hope you join me in my room tonight, I feel a chemical reaction to you, and I don't like taking no for an answer."

I knew my decision would make or break everything. I love to tell a man no who always hears yes. I have a stubborn streak about me, and didn't want him to think I was just another of his sycophants who would do whatever he suggested.

I didn't answer his question, I just smiled and said, "It's getting late. Hopefully I will see you at the pool tomorrow."

Gianni didn't seem to mind that I turned down his offer at all. All of a sudden, he got a twinkle in his eye and gestured to the waiter. He ordered a bottle of champagne and took my hand.

"Well darling, I would like to show you my second favorite thing to do in this hotel other than make love to a beautiful woman."

He grabbed the champagne and two glasses in one hand, and my hand in the other. We ran out of the bar and into the lobby. We started walking up the grand marble stairs, and he stopped halfway up to the top.

"They hate when I do this, but they never stop me."

With that, he leapt from the middle of the stairs up into the air and grabbed onto the massive lobby chandelier on his way down. He was swinging back and forth like Tarzan and singing *I'm in the Mood for Love*! I couldn't believe my eyes! I felt like I was in a scene from a movie except it was really happening!

He jumped off the chandelier and landed like a stealth cat on both his feet onto the lobby carpet. He looked at me.

"Your turn." He said.

I jumped off the stairs and onto the chandelier and started swinging like a rock star.
Without a doubt, this was the most exciting night of my life!

Now I *Swing from the Chandeliers* whenever possible!

Betty and the Fur Coat

Seymour Lamb was spending the long Thanksgiving weekend at White Oaks, his Grandfather's estate near Newport. He was a knock-kneed, timid little tenth grader at a boarding school dominated by alpha males or, as he called the mean boys at school, "The Cro-Magnon Death Crew."

He was enjoying his much-needed break from being abused and harassed by his classmates on a daily basis at his boarding school, where he pretty much walked around on pins and needles, trying not to be spotted. He was also loving not wearing his jacket, tight oxford shirt, and noose-like tie.

Since his sister and two brothers were younger than was he, they were on a different school vacation schedule and had not arrived at White Oaks yet. This meant that he could wander around the big house and property as he pleased until his siblings arrived to scrutinize his every move.

Seymour was friends with Gussie the cook, a big African-American woman who always hugged him, gave him cookies, and was his best ally in the big house. She made him a bowl of popcorn and a grilled cheese with a bottle of coca-cola while he hung out in the kitchen and told her about the mean boys at school.

He lazed about the den, switching between channels, 2, 4, and 7. Nothing on. Just some Saturday afternoon Bowling For Dollars!, news, and an old black and white movie with

Bette Davis. He was feeling bored, so he went outside for a walk to see the horses. He fed his favorite horse, Apple Pie, some carrots and some sugar cubes. How he loved this horse! She nuzzled him and whinnied and licked his entire face when he walked into her stall. Before he could even feed her the treats, she gave him the closest thing possible to a human hug from a non-homo sapien. He often felt Apple Pie was his best friend. She loved him. He loved her. She didn't judge him or bother him; she was just there to give the best kind of love he had ever felt. Whatever bond they shared made him wish he could always be with her and near her, not wasting his time at school, especially his school, which was full of rotting maggots called students.

After riding Apple Pie for about an hour, he tucked her back into her stall, washed her, brushed her, and gave her a sweet, soft kiss goodbye on her velvety nose. He meandered into the house, even though he knew no one except the staff was there yet, and nothing was on TV. He didn't even feel like reading his favorite comic book, or the Playboy he stole from his father's office last month.

So, Seymour just lay on the bed of the red bedroom; it was not even *his* room, just a room where he was assigned if he was lucky. It was decorated with an all red, Oriental theme with the same Scalamandré fabric with red Chinese lanterns and little Chinese people on the wallpaper, the draperies and the bedspread. There were many small yet elegant touches throughout the room that he loved. There was a small Cartier red lacquer clock on the bedside table, an old map of Shanghai in a gold bamboo frame above the bed, and a little brass lamp shaped like a crazy monkey, holding the light part of the lamp in his monkey hand. All of these little quirky touches made Seymour feel cozy in the red room, which made him feel better. He loved the en-suite bathroom, where he could lollygag in the bathtub and still see the TV on the bureau at the same time. Most of the other bedrooms in his grandfather's house did not have a private bathroom, so this made holidays with his overbearing family more bearable. The TV was an old black and white RCA with rabbit ears, but where it was sitting near the window gave it pretty decent reception compared to the other TVs in the house. There were lots of old books to read on the shelves above the desk, old family photographs in albums, and ashtrays from different countries his grandfather had travelled to.

Out of nowhere Seymour smelled a cigarette burning. It smelled like a Chesterfield. He jumped out of bed to make sure there was not a fire, since a maid at his own house had died in a tragic ball of flames in her red Dr. Denton pajamas from a cigarette ash that was still burning.

In the hallway, he definitely smelled cigarettes, and then he saw a column of smoke going up to the third floor.

He said, "Hello, hello, who is there?"

He didn't hear a sound, but then he saw a flurry of a mink coat, long legs in fishnet stocking and heels, and a woman's perfectly manicured, slim hand holding a Chesterfield indeed.

"Hi, what's your name?" The woman said.

"I'm Seymour."

"Well, hello Seymour, I'm Betty. I'm a friend of your grandfather's. I'm here for the weekend."

"Me too," said Seymour.

"Well, maybe we can friends," replied Betty.

Betty beckoned Seymour up the stairs to the third floor.

"Come into my room, I want to show you something," she purred.

He was wearing his favorite old Brooks Brothers blue and gold striped pajamas, which were a little shabby, but still his favorite. He was embarrassed to be wearing his old comfy bathrobe which was white fluffy terry cloth, and had hand-painted Peter Rabbit bunnies all over it. The bathrobe was from The Women's Exchange in New York from years ago that still fit him. He couldn't bear to part with the bathrobe, because his grandmother had bought one for him and all his siblings on a super fun-packed weekend trip to New York. Plus, it still fit him and even though it could have been bigger, he loved it and knew he wanted to keep it forever.

Seymour's mind was wandering. He didn't know how to answer Betty. He was scared. But he was also intrigued. He had never seen such a gorgeous, glamorous woman - especially not down the hallway in his grandfather's house!

Seymour croaked, "What do you want to show me?"

Seymour summoned up the courage to go into Betty's room, he sat on the bed, and Betty handed him a red crocodile photo album filled with pictures of her and his grandfather. She sat on the bed beside Seymour, and her mink coat opened slightly, revealing one of her voluptuous breasts, and a flash of her black lace panties.

She opened a square, green monogrammed Goyard case with the initials B.A. on the front. Betty Anton. Her personal travel bar. She mixed two gin martinis and handed one to Seymour. Though hesitant, he tasted it. He wanted to spit it out because it tasted like rocket fuel, but he swallowed the mixture.

Seymour told her, "It is fantastic, thank you. What is it anyway?"

"Gin martini," Betty declared.

Betty looked at the Tiffany grandfather clock standing in the corner of her room, striking out the hour.

"I have to get dressed and go meet your grandfather now! Come back later."

Seymour had such a mix of emotions after he left her room. He felt exhilarated, almost on fire, his head was dizzy and his feet were wobbly. He definitely wasn't going to tell his brothers about Betty. He was going to keep Betty all to himself.

Seymour went back to the Red Room, *his* room for the long weekend, he told himself. He laid down on the bed and grabbed the box of matches out of the ashtray. The Knickerbocker Club, one of his favorite places in New York - stuffy atmosphere, but great cheeseburgers, they also had the best matches that would light on the first try every time. No rubbing on your hair required. He lit a match and then watched it burn out. He lit about five more matches and let them just burn away. Seymour felt bored and lonely.

He wandered downstairs into the children's dining room, where a silver tray was laid out for him since he was still the only non-grownup here. He found an old Wall Street Journal, and sat down at his spot. He lifted the cover off his tray, and there was his favorite sandwich - a bacon, lettuce and tomato on toast with lots of mayonnaise. There was a side of sliced peaches, some less than fresh radishes and a slice of blueberry pie. He ate the whole sandwich, the pie, but nothing else. He was finishing leafing through the movie section of the old paper when he heard a scream from the next room. He jumped out of his chair, ran to the adjoining wall and put his ear as close to the wall as possible.

He could hear muffled yelling, and his grandfather was saying, "Betty just calm down."

Betty screamed, "Well, I planned the wedding and we can't cancel it now."

She stormed out of the dining room slamming the door behind her. Seymour could hear her crying from the other room.

Seymour cracked open the door between the children's dining room and the big dining room and saw his grandfather still sitting at the table, sipping his red wine, eating dessert and reading a newspaper like nothing at all had happened. Seymour didn't open the door to speak to his grandfather. He ran up the back stairs to the third floor to find Betty and try to console her.

Betty was pacing the floor of the bedroom, with a new martini and Chesterfield in her hand, as she cried violently. Seymour walked in and put his hand on her shoulder. She nestled into him and wept.

"What's wrong?" Seymour asked.

"I have just had enough!" Betty answered through her tears.

Seymour didn't ask anything more, he just rubbed her back and tried to make her feel better.

He ran to his room and pulled out a box from his suitcase. It was a box of French chocolates he was saving for his sister, but he wanted to give them to Betty instead. He walked back into Betty's room and now she was taking all of her clothes out of the dresser and putting them into her big suitcase.

He gave Betty the chocolates and they had another martini. Seymour barely took a few sips, because he was starting to feel really dizzy. Betty had at least two more martinis, and they finished all of the chocolates together. She took off her clothes and got under the covers of the huge Chippendale four poster bed.

"Come lay down with me and read me a story," Betty suggested, gesturing to the bookcase.

"What do you want me to read?" asked Seymour, quizzically.

"Anything," Betty quipped.

He grabbed *The Good Earth* by Pearl S. Buck. He slid under the covers with all of his clothes on and started reading.

He left Betty's room two hours later, his life forever changed.

Seymour went back to his room and took a long hot bath and read a little more of *The Good Earth*. Somehow, after the time he spent with Betty, Wang Lung and O-lan just couldn't hold his interest at all. He decided life in America was pretty good. He put on his old pajamas and got into bed. That night he didn't sleep very well and had fitful dreams, he thought he was hearing noises, yelling and conversations throughout the long night.

When he woke up police and fire trucks were all over the property. All of the people who worked on the estate, maids, chauffeurs, gardeners, and even the neighbors were staring at the small lake in the backyard. His grandfather was smoking a cigar and yelling at the nearest policeman. He asked his grandfather what was happening but received no reply at all.

Seymour ran back into the big house and into the kitchen. "Gussie, what's happening?" he inquired.

"Lord have mercy, that crazy Betty was mad and she drove your Grandad's prize Rolls Royce into the lake! That woman is off her rocker! Crazy as a loon! She done planned a wedding without asking him or him proposing - he said cancel it and she went out of her right mind. She drove that beautiful car into the lake in the middle of the night - can you believe that?" squealed Gussie.

Seymour laughed to himself as he pictured Betty in her fur coat jumping out of the Rolls before it went sailing into the water.

Seymour went back upstairs and crept into Betty's room. To his delight, the room was still heavy with the aroma of her Guerlain perfume. He slipped under the covers and fell asleep with a smile on his face.

I Want to Marry Sting

It was a beautiful early autumn afternoon in New York. You know, one of those days that makes you think about Holden Caulfield wandering around Central Park or Jackie Onassis walking down Fifth Avenue in her big black sunglasses. The sunlight was twinkling off the Time Warner buildings and you couldn't ask for a more perfect day.

Sting (The Demigod of the Western Hemisphere) lives in a gorgeous limestone building on Central Park West. I won't give you the exact address because everyone needs their privacy. But I have been stalking him for years.

On this gorgeous, perfect New York day, I was passing by Sting's limestone palace/building when I thought I caught a glimpse of him getting into the back of a black nondescript GMC sport utility vehicle.

My apartment coincidentally, happens to be right around the corner from Sting's limestone tower in the sky. So after the first time I saw him, I made it a habit whenever I had an extra few minutes, to take a detour and check out his building if possible.

I mostly thought about Sting in the car though, since I always wondered why he - a musical legend for decades, (and The Demigod of the Western Hemisphere), does not have his own SiriusXM station, while someone like Pitbull does.

Sometimes on my way to a morning jog in Central Park, I would even wink at his doorman and say "Tell Sting I said hi."

Most days I didn't see anything, but on a few glorious occasions I saw him going into or out of his limestone palace.

After seeing him around New York several times but not actually knowing him, and for someone as well known as Sting is, I felt like he was a fairly down to earth, cool person. Nary a bodyguard insight, and most of the time he wasn't even sporting any type of a movie star/rockstar disguise a.k.a. dark sunglasses and baseball hat pulled over the face.

One day, on my jog through the park, I took a detour to pass in front of his building as usual, and noticed that he left the building shortly before I arrived and started walking across the street on the Central Park side of Central Park West. Naturally, I followed. I tried to look like a normal jogger and not a crazy fan/stalker/starstruck freak or rabid teenager in love with him.

He was dressed all in black-some kind of supersonic, sleek, astronomical workout gear. The kind of clothing only available to demigods of the Western Hemisphere, not available at your local Niketown or Lululemon for the rest of us.

I was trying in my brain to desperately figure out a way to meet him again.

I have met him several times before. With my friend at the Madison Avenue restaurant Nello, I said hello while he was dining with Richard Grant and his wife. He was very gracious, in fact, even chipper I would say. I also met him when his daughter who is an up-and-coming budding rocker with a lot of talent, was doing a smallish concert at the Armani store in SoHo. Again he was very accessible, very gracious, very affable and willing to meet and greet with anyone who approached him.

That evening I was wearing my favorite Burberry military jacket purchased from the Burberry store in London on Regent Street. I may have looked like an out of place regimental officer, but I adore this jacket and I always feel like fashion should be *fun,* not serious. Plus the jacket is a real conversation starter everywhere and makes people smile.

Sting said, "Nice jacket" at the concert when I walked by. So I reminded him we had just met at Nello, and we also met at Artpark when he was doing a concert there and because I was on the Board of Directors and had amazing front row seats. We chatted for a while and I was very impressed with his nonchalance. (Okay, I was in love and melting).

So, as I was making my way up Central Park West, I wondered if he would recognize me, I had my long blonde hair in a ponytail and it was bouncing around while I jogged. I decided I would show off my athletic skills and jog a little faster than him, and passed him and his own slow but steady jog.

I tried to think of a way where I could meet him again in a fun and cheeky way instead of just saying, "Hi, remember me?"

So after I was jogging in front of him for about five minutes I fell to the ground and feigned an ankle sprain.

As I hoped but did not totally expect, he stopped and asked, "Are you Okay?"

I said "It really hurts," and started rocking back-and-forth holding my ankle.

I just had this idea pop into my head while I was jogging, as I had recently seen my all time favorite film, *Wuthering Heights* with Merle Oberon and Laurence Olivier. Cathy falls on the wall of the estate of Edgar, while the dogs are chasing her. She falls to the ground, prostrate, while Edgar picks her up and carries her into a lavish guest room to convalesce. Edgar is clearly smitten with Catherine.

I was hoping Sting would envision me as a wounded lassie and feel compelled to take me home and take care of me.

He seemed genuinely concerned about my injury and asked me if I needed him to accompany me to the Emergency Room. I told him my ankle felt much better, and then he invited me up to his apartment for tea and to see his Henry Moore sculpture.

His butler opened the door for us and was a calming presence. If one was in the position to hire a butler, it would definitely be this man. He reminded me of the The Chief Steward in Wes Anderson's film *The Darjeeling Limited,* he looked exactly like the actor, except without the turban. Same face, same demeanor, same beard. Maybe it was an Indian priest in disguise if it wasn't Waris Ahluwalia - whoever he was, he had such an air of happiness, grace and inner beauty you just wanted to be near him.

Sting nodded to him and said "Hey Mr. Pink." I found it interesting that Sting was the employer and using the title "Mister" to address his employee. But that's just what Demigods of the Western Hemisphere do.

Mr. Pink proceeded to bring us tea on gorgeous green and gold Limoges china, Sting said it was Da-Hong Pao tea. This tea was absolutely delicious, and the whole tea ceremony he performed for me was very spiritual and almost a religious experience. I am not very schooled in the world of tea, I love Twinings chamomile and the occasional Earl Grey. Sting was more than happy to recount the long, storied history of the Da-Hong Pao tea to me, and did so in a cheerful but fun way, so I didn't feel like a tea plebeian. He told me how this tea dates back to the Ming Dynasty and is a national treasure in China. He said "a friend" procures it for him every month. He told me most tea is ruined with preservatives for shipping to the west, that most of the good tea leaves are reserved strictly for the dignitaries in China, and that tea goes bad after a few months.

I nodded and tried to soak in all this new knowledge, but I was staring at his Charvet blue eyes, his toned arms, and his hair which was shaved tight to his head like a private in the army. This made the veins in his temples seem to bulge and while he was regaling me with the secret tea history, I was only half listening. He also told me that the human body needs vitamins and
exercise everyday, and that certain tea is a like a vitamin for the body.

He had wet armpits, and I didn't ask, but guessed that he eschewed antiperspirant since it is healthy and natural for the body to perspire. He had several beads of sweat on his forehead and temple, which were also distracting me from the tea conversation. I think I said "interesting" and "cool" a thousand times, but he didn't notice. He loved telling me about the tea and his artwork.

I was checking out the eclectic, sleek and funky decorating in the rock star lair surrounding me. The walls of the living room were hot pink, there were three guitars on stands in one corner, four large Julian Schnabel portrait paintings on the walls that looked like they were talking to each other, two large red silk sofas put together in a vee, I was on one, Sting was sitting cross-legged on the other. He was now wearing an old Roy Orbison t-shirt with holes in it, baggy tan cargo parachute pants, and was barefoot. He was so calm, so serene and he looked at least twenty years younger than his actual age. Gorgeous.

Next, Sting took me out on the terrace to see the Moore. It reminded me of two other Moores I love - the glorious *Bronze Form* outside of the new Getty museum in Los Angeles, and my favorite, *Knife Edge Two Piece* at Kykuit, (also in London and Vancouver). He said his Moore was his favorite piece in his entire worldwide art collection. He was stroking the sides of the female nude bronze figure, and gestured for me to feel it as well. It was cold but warmed to my touch, and felt like smooth silk even though it was metal and weighed several tons.

Before we said goodbye, Sting gave me a box of his favorite candles. He instructed me to turn off all the lights at night, just use a candle and close my eyes and breathe. Sting also said I should try yoga alone at night, by the light of one candle.

Since that afternoon, Sting and I became friends and we go for jogs in Central Park together whenever our schedules allow. Now he is number three on my speed dial.

Prada Shoes

FADE IN

EXT. - THE TUSCAN COUNTRYSIDE - DAY
Sweeping Views of the countryside. We hear a young man's voice with a strong Italian accent. An Italian aria is playing.

GINO (V.O.)
I was born in the beautiful countryside of Tuscany. After I was turned into the finest leather in the world, I became a heavenly pair of Prada high heel shoes.

EXT. - GIGANTIC FREIGHTER CROSSING THE ATLANTIC

GINO (V.O.)
Then I went on a big boat to the United States. To New York City, and then to Bergdorf Goodman---the BEST department store in the whole city.

INT. - SHOE DEPT OF BERGDORF'S, ASTRUD GILBERTO IS FLOWING OVER THE SPEAKERS DENOTING JUST HOW HIP THIS PLACE IS.

POV - WE SEE NOTHING OF THE ROOM BUT PEOPLE FROM THE KNEES DOWN

GINO (V.O.)
(UPBEAT)
My first day in a new country and a new store, and everybody wants to try me on!

WE SEE A HEAVYSET WOMAN'S FEET, YOU CAN TELL SHE IS AN OLDER WOMAN...

                MRS. BAKER
(Total nasal voice) I love these, they're fabulous!

              RICHARD (FASHION QUEEN)
              Yes, I'll get them for you Mrs. BAKER

                  GINO (V.O.)
OH NO! Pleeeeeeaaaassseee! Don't try me on! Don't buy me!

MRS. BAKER CRAMS HER FAT FEET INTO THE PRADAS

                GINO (CONT'D)
Oh God! The smell! I can't take it, and NO pedicure, and she's so heavy my heels will break off! No - please no!

                  MRS. BAKER
Oh Richard, they hurt my toes! I can't stand it! Take them away...

                      GINO
                    Thank God!

NEXT WE SEE A YOUNG GIRL'S FEET WALKING INTO SHOE DEPT. WITH BEATEN UP SNEAKERS

                     TAMMY
I think these are really cool (Pradas)

                    RICHARD
                  What's your size?

TAMMY
Nine

WE HEAR TAMMY CHATTING ON HER CELL PHONE WHILE SHE PACES BACK AND FORTH IN THE PRADAS

TAMMY (CONT'D)
Oh shit, I forgot I owe an extra month's rent, I'll ask my dad to float me a loan...

GINO
Oh, she's just a teenager! She will not appreciate my beauty, my workmanship. And the horrible purple glitter pedicure - no taste! And she can't afford me!

TAMMY
Thanks sir, but nine hundred is just too steep...I'll wait for them to go on sale.

RICHARD
Yes, Miss.

THE NEXT CUSTOMER COMES BOUNDING IN...SHE'S A ROCKER TYPE LIKE A YOUNG MADONNA WITH A BOOMING VOICE AND GRUNGY FLIP-FLOPS. HER PEELING BLACK PEDICURE IS POUNDING ACROSS THE SHOE DEPT. AND SHE THROWS OFF HER HANDBAG (A PACK OF CAMELS SPILLS OUT) AND CHUCKS HER FLIP-FLOPS

TREENA
I need like twenty pairs of SUPER high kick ass heels for my next tour, I'm a nine.

RICHARD
Yes, I'll bring you everything in your size right away.

GINO
NO, NO, NO! She's all wrong for me, she will just put out a cigarette with me and spill vodka and red bull on me! She will not appreciate me, she won't even know I exist in her closet!

WE SEE TREENA TRYING ON TONS OF SHOES, WHILE HER STYLIST SAYS, YES, NO, TOO SLUTTY, TOO SUBURBAN ETC.

STYLIST
Yellow - too slutty, black platforms - yes, red sandals - yes, purple heels - no, black Pradas – yes.

GINO
NOOOOO - Please!

TREENA
Nah - they're too conservative.

GINO
Thank you! Phew, that was close!

WE SEE A BEAUTIFUL YOUNG LADIES LEG'S WALK INTO THE SHOE AREA. PERFECT LEGS, KNEE LENGTH BLACK SKIRT, IMPECCABLE RED PEDICURE

HAYLEY
May I try these in a nine?

GINO

Oh yes! FINALLY!!! She is perfect!

HAYLEY (CONT'D)
These are just gorgeous, the stitching, the patent leather, the heel... Ooohhh! I absolutely adore these shoes!

GINO
YES, YES, YES! Pick me! Please, please, please take me home!

HAYLEY ADMIRES HER FEET AND THE SHOES IN A MIRROR...AS SHE WALKS BACK AND FORTH IN THE SHOE DEPT.

GINO
Look at her pedicure! Nice! Amazing mile-long legs - she's divine!

HAYLEY
I'll take them.

GINO
Oh my God! I can't believe how lucky I am! A young and beautiful woman is taking me home!

HAYLEY
I'll actually wear these now, I have a big meeting in a few minutes.

EXT - HAYLEY WALKING DOWN FIFTH AVE. AS "LONDON" BY LILY ALLEN PLAYS WE SEE HAYLEY WALK INTO AN OFFICE BLDG.

INT. - A LONG CONFERENCE TABLE, WITH THE FEET OF THREE MEN (IN SUITS AND DRESS SHOES) AND

THE FEET OF A WOMAN WEARING A PANTSUIT AND SENSIBLE SHOES, SITTING WITH HAYLEY

            HAYLEY (CONT'D)
Well, that was a great quarterly report, thank you everyone. Now, let's discuss the bonus figures.

CAMERA IS PANNING ALL THE SHOES UNDER THE CONFERENCE TABLE - THEY ALL HAVE THEIR OWN VOICE...

           BLACK TASSEL LOAFERS
              (TO GINO)
    Well Mr. Fancy Pants, you're new here.

                GINO
Yes, I am from PRADA. (Slowly and proudly) Where are you from? JC Penney?

          BLACK TASSEL LOAFERS
Very funny! I'm a Stuart Weitzman classic men's loafer, about four hundred bucks - you snob!

             BROWN BUCKS
I'm J. CREW - hey he's just outta college, and I'm a very respectable piece of footwear - made in Italy to boot!

    WOMAN'S SENSIBLE SHOE (RELUCTANTLY)
         I AM from JCPenney...

ALL THE OTHER SHOES LAUGH HYSTERICALLY.

INT - DAY GYM LOCKER ROOM

HAYLEY
Yes, Kim, we are having another date tonight, I think
like him.

HAYLEY PUTS THE PRADAS INTO HER GYM LOCKER AND SLAMS IT SHUT

GINO
I hate being in this... CAGE! Almost a prison! It smells like a dirty gym sock in here. HELP! I'm getting claustrophobic! I need AIR! I need light!

LOCKER DOOR OPENS. "FREEDOM" BY GEORGE MICHAEL PLAYS.

GINO (CONT'D)
Let me out! (GASPING FOR AIR!) YES, that's better!

INT. HAYLEY'S APT. - A LOFT IN MURRAY HILL WITH A BIG CLOSET "CAPE COD KWASSA KWASSA" BY VAMPIRE WEEKEND IS CRANKED UP WHILE SHE PRIMPS AND GETS DRESSED FOR HER DATE

GINO
Please, oh please---wear ME tonight!

HAYLEY PULLS UP THIGH-HI WOLFORD FISHNET STOCKINGS, AND SLIPS ON THE PRADA SHOES

INT. CHIC NYC RESTAURANT (Le Coucou) WE SEE HAYLEY'S LEGS CROSSED AND HER PRADA SHOES UNDER A PRIME TABLE NEXT TO A GUY IN KHAKIS AND GUCCI LOAFERS

GINO

, you are Gucci?? ...so 1995, so
ton, so OVER.

                    UCCI LOAFER
              s? Yawn, yawn. You don't impress me-
              e a $5500 pair of Manolo haute couture
                         pumps.

                         GINO
How do you say "Screw You" in Italian? I forgot! But I am
                     ignoring you!

SHOT OF THE COUPLE'S SHOES PLAYING FOOTSIE
UNDER THE RESTAURANT TABLE AS THEY EAT
DESSERT
                    GINO (CONT'D)
              GET OFF ME! You clumsy idiot!

                    GUCCI LOAFER
                   What? I can't help it!

                         GINO
                    You smell AWFUL!

                    GUCCI LOAFER
              Yeah I know - mothballs and cedar!

                         GINO
                      You are vile!

INT. CUT TO HAYLEY'S COUCH THEY ARE HAVING A
NIGHTCAP SHE'S SITTING ON HIS LAP AND THEY
ARE PASSIONATELY KISSING...

                    GINO (CONT'D)
                  She's too good for him!

                  GUCCI LOAFER
He's had better---last week he had Paris Hilton!

                      GINO
                     TRASH!

THE PRADAS AND THE GUCCI LOAFERS WALK FROM THE COUCH TO THE BEDROOM...HAYLEY AND THE DATE RIP EACH OTHERS' CLOTHES OFF, AND WE SEE THEM LAND ALL OVER THE FLOOR, EXCEPT FOR HAYLEY'S FISH NET STOCKINGS AND PRADA HIGH HEELS...HAYLEY AND HER DATE ARE "DOING IT", WHILE THE XX CRANKS IN THE BACK-GROUND...ALL WE SEE IS HER PRADA SHOES, AND HIS BARE FEET MOVING UP AND DOWN BETWEEN THEM...

                 GINO (CONT'D)
                     Oh yes!

                    HAYLEY
OH MY GOD!! (MOANING IN ECSTASY) YES, YES, YES!!!!!!
                    GINO
               YES!!!!!!!!!!!!

WE HEAR HAYLEY CLIMAXING...

                    HAYLEY
               AHHHHHH!!!!!!!

                    GINO
Thank GOD Mrs. Baker didn't buy me!!!!!!!!!!!!!!!!

FADE TO BLACK.

Salinger and Lebowitz

Fran Lebowitz was having lunch with a friend at Odeon. She went outside for a cigarette. A woman with a stroller passed by and coughed and rolled her eyes at the plume of smoke.

"Fuck you lady - I didn't blow my smoke at your ugly baby!" Lebowitiz says, as she flicks her cigarette into the street and goes back into the restaurant.

She sits back down with her friend and says, "Everyday I fucking hate New York more and more. I miss the bad old days when you could do whatever you wanted to, whenever you wanted to. It was more civilized to dodge bullets in The Bowery than be so god-dammed politically correct all the time you can't even enjoy any aspect of life anymore."

Friend, "Fran, where would you move?, L.A.? You abhor everything about L.A. Colorado? You hate granola kids, patchouli, and fresh air. In all practicality, they only place you could possibly exist other than New York would be somewhere in Europe or the moon."

Lebowitz, "Well, anyplace would be better than this dump." She throws fifty dollars down on the table, "No, don't get up."

Lebowitz storms outside Odeon, she looks up, puts her hand out and feels rain. She doesn't have an umbrella, so she takes the newspaper out from under her arm and tents it above her head. She thinks to herself, why bother?

Lebowitz barely washes or grooms her hair, she could actually care less if it gets a little or a lot wet. Sometimes she thinks about doing something radical like just shaving it all off for shock value. However, since Sinead, Brittany and the chick from Billions shaved their heads as females, no one seems to care anymore. If it wouldn't shock or offend anyone, then what's the point?

She turns and stomps down West Broadway in the rain. Parents with strollers and tourists pass by her hogging "her" sidewalk. She grumpily turns right onto Thomas Street, navigating her way hither and thither Tribeca. She barely looks up or around, she knows the pavement so well. So well, it is like a part of her DNA.

Out of nowhere a monolithic, MTA double length bus comes barreling up to - and rolls over Lebowitz. That's all she remembers.

The next thing she knows, she approaches a door with a sign on the front that says "No Phonies." She didn't know what that was supposed to indicate, but she was compelled to knock on the door. A forty-something, dark haired, skinny man answered the door.

The man exclaimed emphatically, "Hello Ms. Lebowitz, I've been waiting for you!"

"Waiting for me? Who are you?" Asked Lebowitz.

"Jerry Salinger."

"You mean J.D. Salinger?"

"Yeah, that's me last time I checked."

Lebowitz, "Holy shit. You're my idol! Where are we? New Hampshire?"

"No Ms. Lebowitz, we are in Heaven."

"Heaven? No way!" Lebowitz is flabbergasted.

"Indeed," says Salinger.

"I can't be in Heaven!" remarks Lebowitz.

"Yet, you are," replies Salinger.

"First of all, I don't believe in Heaven. I have been an atheist since I was seven years old. Secondly, if heaven exists, I wouldn't go there."

Salinger looks at her sympathetically, "Well, it clearly exists so start believing. That's my advice to you. Anyway, it is very nice to meet you, I have to say, I truly admire your writing."

Lebowitz quizzically, "Why the fuck didn't you keep writing?"

"I tried. I also said everything I wanted to say," Salinger explained.

"You tried? You tried? You didn't write jack shit for forty years. I reread your stuff over, and over and over until I practically turned into Mark David Chapman," Lebowitz huffed.

"There was a time and place for my work, then the world changed. New York changed," stated Salinger.

"New York? New York has been the same since the first Astor lived in the first mansion on Fifth Avenue over one hundred years ago, and before that even. Dog eat dog. Keeping up with The Jones' and The Bezos'. New York needed more of your writing. I needed more of your writing."

Salinger, "What about your writing? You wrote two, maybe three great books, then stopped."

"I didn't *stop* Mr. Salinger. I had massive writer's block and suffered from several obscure anti-social maladies. I knew I wanted to be a writer since I was little. I mean, I only became a writer because I read the Happy Hooker when I was a kid, and wanted to fuck with people like her book did."

Salinger, "But you had no excuse! I watched everything you did from up here. You stopped drinking when you were nineteen, you had Ritalin, you had the internet! I had a radio. By the time all the new tech things came out, my writing days were over."

"So, where is St. Peter?"

Salinger, "Look, you made it in here, so you have to put all that religious mumbo jumbo out of your head. Up here it's more like - did you make it through your life without murdering anyone? Are you really a good person inside somewhere? That's what counts up here. That's what makes it heaven."

Lebowitz looks around, sees his 1950's style desk, a *gigantic* gold and silver super sonic futuristic computer, an uncomfortable looking chair, uninspiring artwork on the wall, and a vase of bland flowers.

"A little underwhelming Mr. Salinger," groused Lebowitz.

Salinger incredulously, "Are you kidding? That gadget is like five thousand computers in one! It's called *The Methuselah*, and it is the most advanced computer ever created. All you have to do is think of something and it writes it for you! It does anything and everything for you if you just send it the brainwaves. That's underwhelming?"

Salinger continues, "You have to get used to it. Soon you will love it here."

"What's to love? At least if I went to the other place there would be some excitement - maybe not excitement, but exciting personalities," Lebowitz insisted.

Salinger, "You have already forgotten what you loathed about New York? Rent gouging, homeless people making you feel guilty after a four hundred dollar dinner whereupon you would pay them each twenty dollars, canines peeing on every visible surface that you will walk on with your Gucci lambskin loafers, tourists gawking all over *your* city? Jeff Koons being worshipped for making fifty-eight million on a piece of crap aluminum balloon puppy? That made you seethe. Trust me - Jeff Koons is not getting in up here - ever. Does that make you feel better?"

"Not really Mr. Salinger. I just expected so much more somehow. Am I going to stay here forever?"

Salinger, "We will get to that later. Not to mention the book you never finished. *I Hate New York*. Let's remember the chapter titles. There was;

1. Iceberg Has No Nutritional Value
2. Chewing with Your Mouth Open
3. Urine, Urine Everywhere
4. Paper over Tablecloths - Why?

5. I Want to Strangle Your Entire Family
6. Poison the Mayor

This was a good start, but you never actually finished it. Let's not forget *Exterior Signs of Wealth* either. What happened to that book?"

"Do you have to stay? What if you wanted to defect to, to the other place?"

Salinger explained, "I hated earth so much I was either going to commit suicide, go into an institution or just freak out and go on a killing spree like the assholes down there now. After I published my books, people annoyed me more and more. Any little ordinary thing would just put me over the edge. That's why I moved to New Hampshire, so I could live in peace somewhat. Better to brood in the boondocks than in the big house. Felt like jail to me though. Being cloistered still wasn't enough to squelch my inner rage. I became a crazed hermit, people drove me nuts, absolutely nuts. If I saw someone park like an asshole, I would put a note on their windshield saying, "Learn how to drive you stupid mother fucker!" I became so incensed and focused on the ridiculous minutiae, I typed up a note, made hundreds of xeroxes and kept them in my trunk. I would actually follow bad drivers around until they parked and then leave the note on their car. If I was really livid, I would also let the air out their tires. I was obsessed. People angered me so, and aggravated me so much! I slashed tires, keyed the paint - any type of revenge I could extract on bad drivers somehow made me feel better. I had to get out of there for good. That's why I enjoy heaven. First I dropped out of society, and then I died. That's why I enjoy heaven more than anyone here. I love it."

Salinger explains, "Look Lebowitz, heaven is not exactly the heaven of the bible or fairy tales, but more of just a place to fulfill your dreams and observe denizens of the earth. I have been working diligently on a new book, and could never get quite inspired until I died. The morbidities and evil of planet earth just depressed me and squelched my writing."

Salinger shows Lebowitz his new tome, titled *Franny and Zooey go to Burning Man*. A zen-like comedy. Salinger said, "Once I died, I realized trying to be an intellectual and impress people was pointless in life. Putting all of the phonies and soulless people aside, I finally understood, overall, it was much more important and impressive to make the ever suffering earth dwellers laugh than to try to teach them anything intelligent."

Salinger asks Lebowitz to read his new book, to which she replies, "I would be honored."

Lebowitz reads *Franny and Zooey go to Burning Man* and she can't put it down. She can't stop laughing like a hyena either, for the first time in her life (or afterlife).

Salinger tells Lebowitz that if she doesn't like it in heaven (he shows her through a window porthole a live image of her still trying to be revived by doctors in the ER) that time passes much slower on earth - she is allowed to write a request and if it passes the Heaven Review Board, she may return to earth to finish unfinished business.

Lebowitz answers, "I have avoided interacting with humans my whole life, actually loathing ninety-nine percent of every person I have ever met - why would I ever want to go back to that place?"

She has a few martinis with Salinger and thinks hard about everything that is happening to her. Alcohol and recreational drugs are promoted in heaven, because they make you happy and zippy without any hangovers or ill health effects. She ponders and ponders the thought. "Hell no!" She tells herself. She would rather be married to Harvey Weinstein and Donald Trump at the same time than return to earth and mingle with the unwashed again!

She recalls the thought of not only the way people looked, the way they smelled, the way they tried to impress others and flaunt themselves. Most especially, she hated the way the general populace spoke English or massacred the English language when they tried to express themselves in the written word. Misusing homophones, which practically killed her on a daily basis - those fucking plebeians without a clue! Always confusing synonyms, and blaspheming figures of speech! The abuse of the English language to Lebowitz was more grievous than a human committing a felony.

Salinger, "Well, take your time and think about it. You have quite a bit of time before you make your final decision, and nothing will change on earth. In the meantime, we have some excellent dinner parties to attend with people you will absolutely be amazed to meet!"

Salinger and Lebowitz get into the airlevator near the kitchen, it is like a spaceship, but goes directly from one Heaven cloudpod to the other without a chance of any accidents. There are no accidents or anything unpleasant in Heaven.

They arrive at their destination. It is a spectacular Villa more impressive than King Ludwig's Castle, or Versailles, and Lebowitz is agape.

"Who lives here?"

"Gertrude Stein and Alice B. Toklas," replies Salinger.

They float up the path to the front gate, and to the front doors. The doors are made of gold vapor, and since no one is an unwanted guest in Heaven, they float right inside.

Gertrude and Alice greet them at the door with a Heaven Hug, which is like an orgasm but you just do it with a hug. It is pure and has no sexual connotation, yet is the best feeling one Heavenly being can give another. It is really not something that can be explained, like the immaculate conception, it is a heavenly mystery and it is not questioned.

Lebowitz just cannot believe she is in the company of two of her greatest heroes, and many of their friends who were well known artists on earth, or strived to be. Such a wonderful and unimaginable amalgamation of talent, brains and friendship all in one dining room.

Stein and Toklas are not her heroes just because of their sexual orientation and their ability to live openly and love each other and be completely happy and fulfilled. It is because she can see them, and touch them, and know them. They are a million times better than she ever imagined. Two human beings so loving and so ahead of their time, which is why they have such vast rewards in Heaven.

Salinger, Lebowitz, and the rest of the guests dine on eighteen courses of the finest Lily Pad cuisine, the food of Heaven, which is similar to French food, yet ultimately sinless since calories truly do not exist and are not needed in Heaven. After dinner and dessert, the entire group goes to the billiard room where Stein insists that everyone plays.

Stein, "So Lebowitz, you know you can still go back, right?"

"I was just told. I like it here though. I don't want to go back."

"Well, give it time dear, give it time," said Stein. "You know that Judy Chicago was in Heaven for awhile. She lived with us for a few months, then we encouraged her to go back and fulfill her artistic dreams. As soon as she returned to earth, she started working on The Dinner Party. The rest is history as I'm sure you know. She is going to come back here someday soon though, and we still have her room here for her just as she left it. Our dear friend Hemingway was here for awhile too, sadly, he never returned."

On the way home in the airlevator, Lebowitz tells Salinger that she has decided she will stay in Heaven.

The next morning, while Salinger is at his Karma Floating class, Lebowitz decides to play on the mythical *Methuselah* and reread *Franny and Zooey go to Burning Man*. She sits down in front of *The Methuselah*, and the document opens by itself. In Heaven the technology is light years ahead of earth according to everything Salinger has told her and what she has experienced and seen. Salinger told her that they can't give humans on earth all the technology that exists up here because they would stop evolving. Makes sense.

Lebowitz falls asleep while playing video craps on *The Methuselah* and has a wild dream about returning to earth and becoming the best selling author in history. She wakes up, wipes the drool off her lips (yes, there is drool in Heaven), and frantically searches the drawers of Salinger's desk until she finds what she is looking for. A flash drive. She uploads *Franny and Zooey go to Burning Man* onto the drive and puts it into her pocket.

Lebowitz thinks. The flash drive is palpable in her pocket.

"I like Heaven. I miss my 10,000 books. I miss my friends. I have writer's blockade, but I also have this amazing new story in my pocket," she ponders to herself.

She hastily scribbles a note to Salinger.

"Thanks for everything Jerry - you're a peach. I gotta run but I will see you again someday."

She takes the airlevator back to door that says "No Phonies". She tries to leave at the escalator bay, but the tech detector goes off.

An attendant comes out and asks her to slowly walk through the scanner again. It beeps and the sirens go off again. Another older attendant comes out.

"Fran Lebowitz, God knows you have the flash drive in your pocket. You have two choices - you can give it back and stay here, or take it back to earth with you and never be allowed to return."

Lebowitz announces, "I have to go sir."

She signs all the legal documents stipulating that she may never, *ever* enter Heaven again.

As soon as she gets back to the hospital, she runs out of the Emergency Room in a flurry, to the amazement of the attending physician and nurses at her side trying to revive her.

She tears back to her apartment and she emails her editor her new book.

Just as she hoped but dared not dream, *Franny and Zooey go to Burning Man*, becomes number one on the New York Times bestseller list. It bumps J.K. Rowling right off the list for longevity and sales, and sells 130 million copies in the first few months.

Lebowitz is a newly minted cheerful, if not downright happy, guest on all the late night talk shows. She now regales the audience with stories of how opening her heart to kindness and feeling the light of the universe in her soul changed her life and made her a new person.

"My life is like Scrooge in *A Christmas Carol*. I practically skip the streets of New York now. I am so happy I hate myself!"

The Cowboy of Madison Avenue

I was exhausted, but it a was a gorgeous winter's day and I had just gotten off set early, so I had the whole day to be decadent and stroll around New York. When I say 'off set,' I don't mean I am a movie star, although I hope to be someday before I am ninety. On this day, I was an extra in the Martin Scorsese film *The Irishman*. I was playing a mob wife, so I was all, well, mobbed up. My hair was teased up to kingdom come, I had loads of 70's make-up on; we are talking long false eyelashes, blue eyeshadow, and frosted pink/white lipstick, and enough rouge to kill a drag queen.

We had to report to set in Harlem at 6 a.m. for the Frank Sheeran appreciation night dinner, but when we got there, after spending three hours in hair and make-up, we were told there would be no shooting today, but if you are SAG, you would get paid for a full day.

I took a taxi to E.A.T. on Madison Avenue, to finally have some real food after being on set all week and eating the worst crafty of all time. I sat down at a quiet table by the window, ordered an omelet, a fresh squeezed orange juice (they have the best), and a cappuccino.

The man at the table next to me said, "Excuse me, may I borrow your pepper? I don't have any on my table and there is not a waiter to be seen for miles."

"Of course," I said.

I was reading yesterday's Financial Times because someone left it on the table before I arrived. Sometimes I get so tired of constantly staring into my smartphone, I like to be reminded that the world indeed existed before those handy but hellish devices. I still prefer to read actual books made of paper, and actual newspapers rather than just looking at a screen.

I looked over at the man next to me, and he had the New York Times style section sitting on the chair next to him, but he was not reading it. I asked him if I could borrow it and he said sure. Then I joked and said we could just share everything from our tables because we keep asking to borrow something from the other's table.

I was absolutely famished and literally scarfing down the omelet like I had not had a meal in days. I started choking, and then drank some water and I was fine. I was so embarrassed because I looked like a barbarian in front of this very civilized man dining next to me. He looked very familiar, but I could not place him.

"Easy tiger," he said and laughed after I stopped choking. "Are you okay?"

"Yes, thanks. Went down the wrong highway I think."

"I love your shirt, by the way, you have great taste."

"Thank you, I love tuxedo shirts, I have tons of them and wear them with everything from jeans, to pantsuits, or just with a black blazer and anything else." I looked down at what I was wearing, Ralph Lauren tuxedo shirt, Ralph Lauren black velvet jeans, and an old Ralph Lauren sailing jacket with fireman's metal lobster clasp closures.

"Everything I am wearing is Ralph Lauren, his designs are amazing, flawless and timeless. I have had this jacket since college. His stuff never goes out of style." I said as I continued to wolf down my breakfast.

He stood up, put on a Stetson Diamonte cowboy hat and left with with a very huge smile. "Have a great day," he said, as he pushed his chair into the table.

I just realized who I was scarfing down breakfast in front of - the one and only Ralph Lauren!

He looked fantastic, and I couldn't believe I had no clue it was him, as I blathered on and on like a fool about what great clothes he makes, and probably with a crumb of toast hanging out of my mouth. I was bummed that I missed the opportunity to tell him I love his designs and that I am a big fan, but I guess I actually did without knowing it.

I paid my bill, and went back out onto sunny Madison Avenue. I continued walking down Madison and went into the Polo women's store. I hadn't been in awhile, so I walked in to check it out. I was walking around the second floor when the salesgirl said, "Wow, you are a dead ringer for Ricky Lauren."

"Thank you, that is such a wonderful compliment!" We started talking about the amazing plaid silk blazers that were fit for royalty and she offered me a Pellegrino.

"I am actually looking for a few more tuxedo shirts like this one. Do you have any more? Size four?"

"Try on this blazer while I go check in the back," she said.

Just then, Ralph himself walked in.

"May I borrow your pepper?" He asked.

"Oh my gosh! I didn't realize that was you!" I introduced myself and I think I started blushing.

"I was told you are the spitting image of my wife, so I figured it had to be the woman from E.A.T., " he said as he smiled. "I was delighted with your remarks at the restaurant by the way. Anyway, Ricky is actually here, you should meet her, she would love to meet her twin."

A few minutes later he came back with the most elegant decked out in Ralph - woman you have ever seen on his arm. She was wearing faded jeans, a white poet's shirt, drop dead gorgeous black riding boots, and an stunning black military jacket. Wow, did she look amazing!

We chatted for awhile and I told them I was working on a book of short stories, and showed them pictures of my kids on my phone. They were very affable and sweet. I told them the story of how their personal chef was from my hometown, and I was hosting a cooking club luncheon at my house upstate and the kitchen almost started on fire, but we put it out thankfully. They loved that story.

He told the manager to give me the family discount, and they said goodbye and left arm in arm.

The manager was super cute, and super excited about my book. "We will have a book party for you here when the book comes out! We will have lots of champagne of course and you can wear anything you like from The Collection," gushed Samantha.

I was in the dressing room trying on some outfits, when I looked out the window and saw the cowboy hat again, and the happy couple strolling back up Madison Avenue together.

The Stetson Diamonte cowboy hat was walking off into the sunset with his lady. Yes, it was Ralph.

The Cowboy of Madison Avenue.

I Lost My Underwear at Château Marmont

I was going through a bad divorce, and I always wanted to attend the Oscars, the after parties, and pretty much just be in Los Angeles during Oscar week. For actors and show-biz people, it's like going to the Super Bowl for football fans, the Stanley Cup for hockey fans, or Comic-Con for comic book aficionados.

I didn't really have a plan, so I just bought an airline ticket online and decided I would figure out the rest later. I just knew that I had to get out of town and my American Express card still worked, so what the hell? Why not go for it?

I had a few friends in L.A., but didn't want to impose on any of them for twelve days, so I booked the best room I could find for the best price at the Hyatt Century City. Great location because you can be in Santa Monica or West Hollywood or Beverly Hills within minutes, traffic permitting.

I arrived at my hotel, and I believe it was the biggest trip I ever took alone without my husband, since we always traveled everywhere together and did everything together. After the six-hour flight, car rental hell, two carry-ons and two giant suitcases, and finally jumping into my hotel room bed, I realized I was exhausted and just ordered a hamburger and some chardonnay from room service.

I couldn't wait to explore Los Angeles and meet up with old and new friends, enjoy the sunshine, and the culture. I have about three dear friends who are in the show business world. One is a producer, one is an actor, and one is a writer. I reached out to all of them and told them I needed a ticket to the Academy Awards ceremony. I naively figured one of them would be able to pull some strings and get me a ticket. I just wanted to be a part of all the excitement, glamour and fun even if I was not celebrating working on a nominated film.

Each and every one of my contacts scoffed and said, "No, I cannot get you a ticket to the Academy Awards ceremony!" My friend Herbie said, "You don't even want to go if you are not part of a project that is being nominated, it's like sitting through a boring high school graduation except most of the people are like mummies and pumped so full of Botox they can't smile, laugh or have fun anyway." Herbie said, "What you want to do is go to one or more of the *after* parties. That's where the fun, cool people are and they are relaxed, and celebrating and you would love it."

Herbie said I should try to get into the Vanity Fair party (which was held at the Sunset Tower Hotel at that time), the Elton John party, or the Château Marmont party. Believe it or not, I had the two suitcases that each were bigger than a middle schooler, and I had every outfit for any occasion that may arise, including an African safari, sailing and looking drop-dead gorgeous while being rail meat - yet no gown for Oscar night. I decided when I was packing that if I did score a ticket while in L.A., I would have to get a gown out there and assemble the entire movie star ensemble from scratch. I was literally so stressed out while I was packing and just trying to get the hell out of my house that I couldn't even think about putting together the perfect Oscar night outfit.

All week long, I made phone calls trying to get my name on a list for one of the after parties. Either none of my friends had the right connections, or none of them really *tried*. I made a few calls and decided I would go get a gown, have my hair done, and get really glammed up and try to get into one of the parties.

I went to Saks and Neiman's to no avail - just garish, older lady sequined gowns even a brain dead suburban hausfrau would be not be caught dead in were left at this hour on Oscar day. I didn't have time to hoof it around Rodeo or Melrose searching every designer boutique for a spectacular gown. Barney's was my last hope. I went to the evening wear department, and only found two gowns that were even worth trying on. One was a red silk Valentino silk organza with a plunging neckline and long sleeves. I am not a red person, but the cut and style of the gown were really sexy. The other was a sleek, black sleeveless sheath by Maison Martin Margiela. I didn't own any of his designs, but I liked the understated and elegant Belgian look. I tried on the Valentino gown first - it was just way too mother-of-the-bride or too Mariah Carey like for my palate. I slipped on the MMM gown, which was actually not a dress, but a pair of super slim silk pants built into the gown and covered by skirting in the front and back. Very clever design - it spoke to me. I put the gown on my Barney's charge card and tore outta there to drive back to my hotel and get ready. I had the perfect black patent pumps, and I would figure out the make-up and jewelry that I had to work with.

I stopped at the Beverly Wilshire for a quick blow-dry and Katie pimped out my hair à la Bridgette Bardot and made me look oh-so-glamorous. I was excited to go get ready and see what the night would bring.

When I arrived back at my hotel, it was six o'clock, so I had plenty of time to get ready and then crash the after parties. I showered, shaved my legs, moisturized from head to toe, then began the business of getting decked out in Oscar night worthy style.

Make-up wise, I am pretty basic - I never wear foundation as I was blessed with great skin, a few freckles and no acne my whole life. I also firmly believe foundation makes a woman look too made-up, so corpse-in-a-casket-like, and never natural or beautiful. Foundation makes any woman look older and harsh. Every day, I just moisturize my skin with a basic face cream like Clinique or Lancôme, apply some blush to my cheeks, mascara, a light eyeliner below the bottom lashes, and some pink or red (in the evening) lipstick.

I carry all this make-up in an orange Epi leather Louis Vuitton pochette bag. As I said, when I was packing for this trip, I was just concentrating on getting out the door, last minute packing, without a guarantee of any Oscar festivities. So, I am low key make-up wise; however, when I go to a cocktail party or an event, I either glam up with a little silver liquid French eyeshadow, or Chanel gold eye shadow. Of course, when I looked in the goody bag, no eyeshadow or anything glittery to Hollywood me up! I had nothing, it was Sunday night, and I couldn't go out glam make-up foraging at this hour. Just then I remembered I bought some Lancôme items and received a free make-up bag of mini cosmetics. Maybe, just *maybe*, there was something useful inside. Nothing shimmery, but there was a chunky black Kohl eyeliner I could use on my upper lid Cleopatra style. I held my breath because these endeavors can go so very wrong, and a make-up pro I am not. Thankfully, on the first try, I achieved the subtle Cleopatra look without overdoing it and looking like a trashy hooker.

Next, I put on the sheath. Really stunning. I loved this gown! It was very understated and just needed a dash of oomph and bling at the neck. I love pearls, and have a wild assortment of all sorts of oversized, chunky, and statement pearls. I opened my jewelry pouch to see what I had to work with - one oversized gobstopper pearls, one necklace of three stranded pearls, and two or three other pearl necklaces. At first, I just decided to go with the giant gobstoppers, but then I decided to experiment. People who know me, know that I am not a "less is more" person, I am a "MORE is more" person. So, I added all the other pearls to the gobstoppers, but it just looked messy. Then I took off all the other pearls and wrapped each strand around the gobstoppers one by one. This was a *very cool* effect. It looked like I had a pearl breast plate on, and I adored my "new" necklace! Necessity truly is the mother of invention - or a great emergency fashion statement.

I was all decked out and ready to go into the Oscar crashing night. The three parties of choice to crash were the Vanity Fair party at Sunset Tower, The Château Marmont party, and the Elton John party. I stopped at the bar of my hotel for a glass of chardonnay to go, and jumped into my rented giant black Mercedes SUV to give my party crashing skills a whirl.

The hour was nigh.

I had saved up some pocket money; I had six C-notes in my robin's egg blue silk Tiffany evening bag and an Amex, and I was ready to rock and roll. I drove past the Sunset Tower hotel to do some reconnaissance - not one, not two, but *three* Checkpoint Charlies. I held my breath and pulled up to the first checkpoint. I gave the Neanderthal security guy my real name, then my passport when he asked for ID, and said I was with Owen Wilson (whom I met and kind of knew). I somehow convinced checkpoint number one to let me through. At checkpoint two, no matter what kind of song and dance I gave this security team, I was not getting to the third checkpoint. I didn't even try to bribe the second Checkpoint Charlie linebacker with money, this was *serious* business, and cops were standing next to him.

I pulled away and decided to employ plan B. Every hotel has a back door or two, so I had the C-notes ready to bribe a rent-a-cop and was fairly confident I could pull it off. I cruised around to the back of the hotel, whereupon I saw SIX gigantic security guards! Even I didn't have the finesse to sweet talk and pay off six rent-a-cops! I waited in the back parking lot, staking out the possibilities or rather the non-existent possibilities.

Then I saw Steven Spielberg, Kate Capshaw, and another couple being spirited into the back entrance. There was just *way* too much security to even waste my time trying here. I realized I was not the first gate-crasher with this idea tonight or previous Oscar nights.

Practically right across the street on Sunset Boulevard, sits the Château Marmont. I took a sip of my wine, reapplied my soft pink Chanel lip gloss and pulled up to the tiny driveway and the next rent-a-cop with a clipboard.

"Good evening," I said, giving the rent-a-cop my most charming smile.

"Name," the power-wielding pipsqueak said.

He didn't care if I was Miss America or Princess Grace resurrected from the dead. If I was not on the list, I was dust. I just said I was looking for someone to save face and avoid the whole fake pretending I was even on the list. Pipsqueak told me to move along.

I circled the building. I pulled over by the service door in the back of the hotel. I was sitting in the SUV, doing some Château recon. I was still nursing my wine and trying to come up with a plan to get into this place. I knew there was no hope at the front entrance, and I wanted to have a solid plan before I just tried the terrace entrance. Soon enough I saw a cute little bus boy taking chairs from their storage area and into the back door. I did a quick once over on the face and make-up. Looked good. I decided to take off my giant blue topaz David Yurman ring because it was just a little too much bling. I left it in the storage area between the armrests, grabbed my evening bag and my phone, and decided to go for the gusto. I pulled the giant SUV *way* up onto the side of the hill behind the Château, so it was on a huge angle, probably 90% on the hill, and 10% on the actual road behind Château. It was literally the *only* place to park it since every other spot on the narrow road behind the hotel was cluttered with all the attendee's huge black SUV's. I clicked the lock on the key fob, and hoped and prayed that this baby did NOT get towed.

I walked up to the busboy, smiled, and said "I'll pay you one hundred dollars if you let me in this door."

He was so cute, and so eager to help me, and so nice. He just looked at me and said, "No señorita, you don't have to pay me anything!"

He was so sweet I just wanted to give him a big hug and a kiss! I was so elated! I gave him sixty dollars and told him he had to take it. I lucked out because I was planning on bribing someone with a lot more money than that!

I smiled and waved goodbye to Jorge as I strolled through the garden trying to look like an invited guest instead of an interloper. I asked the hostess where the Oscar party was and she said by the pool which has its entrance by the front door. I moseyed out the front door which leads to the front parking lot and the valet with the Checkpoint Charlie. Standing on the landing of the front door, I looked towards the pool to see - guess what? A publicist with a clipboard of names. Of course.

I decided to be calculated. This was my one and only hope of getting into the Château party, and I just had to figure out a way to get in. I pretended to be on my phone while I schemed in my head. Just then a very handsome, bearded, bald guy in a t-shirt, shorts, flip-flops and eating a bag of Cheetos (I kid you not) approached me.

"Hi, what are you doing?" he said.

I thought, "Who was this character with the flip-flops and Cheetos?"

"Hi, actually I am just trying to figure out a way to sneak into this Oscar party," I said. I didn't have to try to impress Mr. Flip-flops, so I just told him the truth.

He smiled at me and said, "I can get you in."

"*You* can get me in?" I though he was an extra valet driver who lost his uniform.

"Yes, I live here, I can get you in no problem. The staff loves me here."

"You live here?" I asked. "No one lives at the Château anymore," I said.

"Yes, I really live here. My name is Red by the way." Then he kissed my hand.

"I'm Sophia," I said and gave him one of my new ecru Crane calling cards with oval corners and a big S flanked by a laurel wreath.

"Sophia Smith? Sounds like a movie star," he said. "Well you definitely look like a movie star," and smiled at me.

He took my hand and walked me over to the girl with the clipboard. "Hi Skylar, this is my friend Sophia, she's with me."

With that, he pulled me into the pool area. It was still early as far as Oscar parties go, but there was a buzz of people all around the pool. Dapper guys decked out in tuxedos, and starlets and gorgeous babes as far as the eyes could see.

I turned around and looked at Red. "Thank you so much for getting me in here! You made my night!"

"You are very welcome," he said.

"Why don't you go up to your room and put on your tuxedo and come back down to the party?"

"I just moved back to the U.S. from Europe and my tuxedo is in storage, but I have black suit I can put on."

"Yes," I said. "Go up and change and come down, we will have so much fun at this party!"

"Will do." He took my hand again and kissed it goodbye. Mr. Flip-flops might have been wearing a t-shirt and eating Cheetos, but he sure was debonair.

I walked around the pool and the party, scoping out the crowd and to see if I knew anyone. Nope.

The waiters were serving glasses of Cristal, so I sipped one while I gazed upon the scene.
I recognized a few well known faces and started chatting some people up. I went to the side of the pool where a bar was set up and people were smoking. I had a cigarette and started talking to a well known political activist's son, who of course had a screenplay to sell - don't we all?

Then I started talking to several Rock n' Rollers about what an amazing venue The Hollywood Bowl is, how great The Stones still sound, and how all the artists are forever touring now since they don't make much money from selling their music today.

I wandered inside to the area where the party was getting into full swing. I saw all the actors. the director, and the powers-that-be from the film that won the best picture award whooping it up by the bar. I was served another glass of Cristal, and just then Red walked up to the bar.

"Care to dance?" He took me by the hand to the dance floor. An orchestra was playing big band music, there were dozens of giant vases filled with white Casablanca lilies everywhere, and low, romantic lighting. It all lent itself to an old Hollywood vibe. Very chic, very cool, and everyone was in a gleeful, celebratory mood, which made the night even more magical.

Red and I danced the night away! I am not even a dancer, but the evening and the music and the champagne all went to my head and we danced for hours!

The party was thinning out, and we were invited to the after, *after* party. This was in a hotel room bungalow by the pool. I was amazed at the interior of this "room." I had oft heard stories of stars throughout history staying at the Château and imagined the rooms would be the height of Hollywood glamour. Boy, was I wrong! Although the lobby, the bar, and the gardens are elegant and beautiful, the actual hotel rooms are nothing of the sort. The furniture looks like it is from a Goodwill fire sale, there was a kitchenette with a World War II era vintage stove (not the cool type, the ugly type), and a ton of formica only a mother could love. I am not trying to bash the rooms (because I was on cloud nine the entire evening and this was just part of the experience), I was just surprised they weren't updated much more to modern luxury standards. I understand that André Balazs wants to keep the old school Hollywood hideaway feel. It is uber cool and it works.

When we walked into the after, *after* party, there was a D.J. in the corner spinning real records on a turntable. The first thing I heard was the guitar strumming of the intro to The Smiths "Bigmouth Strikes Again." I couldn't believe how amazing this song sounded! I don't know if it was the sound system, the full moon, or the night long imbibing of Cristal, but it was like the first time I heard it and it sounded like the best song in the world. To be truthful, I had overplayed, and overplayed, and overplayed The Smiths through most of the 90's, so I hadn't been able to listen to them for years. But, oh how I loved this song tonight! "Oh sweetness, sweetness I was only joking when I said I'd like to smash every tooth in your head." "And now I know how Joan of Arc felt."

Red and I drank a copious amount of champagne throughout the night. *So much* champagne, in fact, I started to get confused. I looked down at my hand that was formerly sporting the *huge* blue topaz David Yurman ring, and realized it was gone! Zut alors! Within two seconds, the entire nearby staff, the best director, best actor, and everyone else was looking high and low for my ring! Nowhere to be found!

I felt like crying, but realized that it was insured, and also realized it was not the end of the world. I imagined either it had slipped off due to heavy champagne consumption, or else I removed it to wash my hands at some point in the evening and left it on the edge of a sink.
Either way it was gone!

We stayed at the after party for a little while longer then I looked at Red and said, "Well I'm off."

Red said, "Don't go, I don't want you to leave, and you can't drive back to your hotel."

"I'll get an Uber, I'm exhausted and I need to sleep," I said.

"Just come up to my room, I have a suite and you can stay in the bedroom and I'll stay in the living room," suggested Red.

I don't know why I was trusting a practical stranger who wore flip-flops, but I went upstairs with him.

He kissed me and I said, "Goodnight now." I was wearing a heavy to the floor silk gown, and obviously was not going to sleep in that.

"Do you have pajamas I can borrow?" I asked.

"No," said Red. He gave me a well-loved and faded Dartmouth t-shirt and a pair of tighty whities.

"Don't you have boxers?" I asked.

"Nope. Sorry just briefs." Said Red.

I locked the bedroom door (just to be on the safe side), slid under the covers and fell fast asleep.

When I awoke the next morning, I asked Red to move my car for me to the valet so I could shower and not worry about it being towed as all of the LAPD was now freed up to enforce parking violations.

Red said he didn't feel comfortable moving my car, and I somehow got the feeling that he just didn't want to leave me alone in his lair. Did I just spend the night in a hotel room with a drug lord? An arms dealer? A hit man? An FBI agent? I didn't try to figure it out, I just wanted to get the heck out of there.

I went back into the bedroom to change and somehow couldn't find my underwear. I couldn't remember if I had hid them under my gown or where they went, but I didn't bother scoping them out. I was going commando under the MMM gown and had no alternative for shoes save the five inch Manolo's I wore the previous night. I seriously looked like I was walking the walk of shame when I went to the front door and gave the attendant my car key and told him where it was parked.

When he pulled up to the entrance, I was so excited to see that the car hadn't been towed! Not only that, when I jumped in, I opened the compartment in between the two front seats and my David Yurman ring was inside! BONUS!

I was so thrilled, I gave the attendant a twenty dollar tip and a gigantic hug and practically picked him up off the ground. I think I made his day. He certainly made mine!

All in all, it was a *very* memorable evening. I may have lost my underwear at The Château Marmont, but I was not the first. In fact, a few noteworthy people have also lost their unmentionables at the Château, including Errol Flynn, James Dean, Jean Harlow, Clark Gable, F. Scott Fitzgerald, Mae West, Humphrey Bogart, Audrey Hepburn, Marilyn Monroe, Howard Hughes, Elizabeth Taylor, Natalie Wood, Dennis Hopper, Johnny Depp, Billy Idol, Jim Morrison, and, of course, John Belushi and Helmut Newton, rest their souls.

Tree Killer

I want to tell you about my friend's Christmas tree.

Like how it began as a mere decoration in his apartment. But he became a little more enraptured with the glorious flora everyday. The invigorating pine scent would fill his nostrils every time he entered the living room. It made him happy, and reminded him of his uncle taking him bow and arrow hunting in Muskoka when he was a kid.

It also made him think about nature, the environment, and feeling closer to the planet and its creator. "A thing of beauty is a joy forever". This quote passed through his brain every time he walked by his tree.

He watered the tree daily (usually at night since he was always running late in the morning), and added a sugar cube to the water in the tree stand, as the guy at Chelsea Market recommended this to lengthen its "shelf life" and hinder the needles from falling off too fast.

He also felt guilty at times, for being responsible for chopping down a living thing. In a way, he felt like he was raping and pillaging the planet. Maybe he should have donated the eighty bucks to a soup kitchen instead of wasting it on a tree. Frivolous. Useless. In the end, pointless.

It will just be kicked to the curb like an unwanted lamp when someone moves out of their first apartment. Rotting in the street, abandoned, just to be peed on by a bum or a passing dog. Its fate will only get worse after that. The tree he loved, gazed on so often, admired, enjoyed the aroma of, and made him so fleetingly happy will be taken to a stinky, horrible garbage dump in New Jersey.

He grew to believe he actually robbed the innocent tree of its future. A perfect life in the woods. Just getting bigger and better every year. Watching the lovely cardinal chicks hatch and grow and then fly every spring. Never again.

He began to feel like a criminal whenever he entered the room after the first few glorious guilt free days. He was sure he knew just how Terence Stamp felt in *The Collector*. His tree was like a kidnapped girl, being held hostage in the living room for his own personal twisted pleasure. Like Stamp, he really didn't want to hurt the tree. He just wanted to look at it because it was so pretty.

He also reminded himself of a black market art buyer. No one can know their secret...they can't show off their acquisition to their friends. They can't even keep it out in the open. Only hidden away to be enjoyed all alone. Almost orgasmic in its sinfulness. Such a delight to the senses. The guiltiest of pleasures and getting caught will surely result in jail time. But seeing Munch's work on their very own bedroom wall is worth the risk. He violated the tree in the same way the world is violated by an art theft, stealing a thing of beauty meant to be enjoyed by all, for his own gluttonous pleasure.

He started having nightmares about the tree. In the dream, the tree had eyes, and just cried and cried and cried. Also, a recurring dream where his girlfriend gave him a beautifully wrapped present, and when he opened it, it was a baseball hat with the letters "T.K." embroidered at the top.

Tree Killer.

A Pro Tried to Kill Me at Hotel Costes

I was having a bad summer. I know, people in the Northeast are supposed to relish every single second of summer, but not this summer. An old friend of mine invited me on a tennis trip to the Loire Valley and Paris with a group of business associates. I just had to get out of Dodge, so of course I said yes. Even during the happiest of times, one simply cannot turn down a trip to Paris.

There was quite the crew of characters on this trip. The name of their group is YPTO - Young Presidents Tennis Organization. The YPTO is a group of CEO's who meet to promote business growth amongst their peers. One would imagine all of these gentlemen to be intelligent, glamorous, driven (i.e.: in shape because they are driven, not only in the business world, but driven to work out and be fit), and be the best of the best.

Well, on this trip, other than a few shining stars, were the third string duds of the YPTO tennis world, apparently. There was Big Billy and Little Billy, round and robust Rob, Tony with the wandering eye, and Ace with a head full of empty space. This was just for starters.

Day after day, the guys played tennis and the women, a.k.a. WAGS (wives and girlfriends), explored the city, shopped, worked out, and did girl things. A couple of the devoted

WAGS (one or two out of fifty, let's say), actually stayed at the courts and dotingly watched their significant others hit the tennis ball all day long. NOT me! Since I didn't have WAG status, just friend status, I was free to roam Loire and Paris with my new lady friends at my leisure. We toured many fine chateaux in the Loire, followed by touring the copious vineyards, sampling all the fine Loire Valley wine, and biking around the gorgeous Loire countryside. In Paris, we explored from The Orsay to the belfries of Notre Dame, soaking up the culture day after day. The Louvre, The Picasso Museum, shopping along the Champs Élysées, lunches at Ralph's on Boulevard Saint-Germain - the glorious days were ours to design and we basked in as much French paradise as we could.

The end of our trip to the Loire Valley and Paree was nigh. This was our last night to go out on the town as we pleased - no pri-fixe group dinner with "comme ci, comme ça" wine tonight!

Of course, I decided that we should go (only the cool people) to Hotel Costes as I have been a fan of their house music for years and have all of their albums in my iTunes library. We arrived early for this place, and easily shimmied up to the petite bar among the low velvet slipper chairs, velvet sofas, and crystal chandeliers, where the hippest people in Paris were partying.

I was going to order a white wine or a martini, but then I spied a luscious pink drink in a mammoth champagne flute large enough to bathe in. The bartender was pouring some type of clear liquor, champagne, and another red French liquor into the concoction, topped off with a beautiful violet orchid. I had no idea what it was, but I knew I wanted to drink one - it looked heavenly! I politely asked the bartender what the drink was called and what was in it but she didn't want to take the time to tell me over the loud din of the thumping house music. So I said, "quatre s'il vous plaît." We drank these potent goblets of party fuel all night, and soon strange things began to happen.

We had a table with a bottle of champagne, and were also standing at the bar. Ace, Tony, me, and Big Billy was sitting down at the bar. We were chatting and remarking how amazing it was to be here, halfway across the earth in one of the hippest bars on the planet. Someone pointed out that Scarlett Johansson was in one corner and David Beckham was in the other. We were soaking in the coolness around us and (without being obvious), thrilled to be there. Who, me? Yeah, I rub elbows with ScarJo in Paris ALL the time, so it's practically old hat by now!

Pretty soon, an extremely robust woman with size DDD or maybe LMNOP size gazungas was walking back and forth behind us at the bar. She made an effort to not just graze, but practically tackle Big Billy's entire upper body with her oversized breasts each time she passed. He turned to the three of us and said, "If that prostitute rubs her boobs on me one more time, I'm calling security to have her thrown out of here!"

I asked, "Is that really a prostitute?" I literally had no idea, and I wasn't noticing what she was doing each time she walked by because I was talking to Ace and Tony. Big Billy started cringing and making faces every time she walked by and we were practically on the floor seizing with laughter.

She heard us saying, "Why would they let hookers into a place like this? The drinks are sixty euros each!" For some reason she didn't like me. She zeroed in on my face with some type of X-Men, X-ray-outer-space-laser-vision-stare. She didn't like the fact that we were calling her a prostitute and laughing about the whole thing. She also didn't like the fact that Big Billy was just not interested in her whatsoever. Big Billy was talking to me in a nonchalant way, and the Queen of the Night came up to me and screamed in my face.

"I can't believe they let scrawny, flat chested, American women in this bar." Her face was seething with anger; the fangs had emerged.

I decided to ignore her completely as I certainly wasn't going to get into a shouting match or fisticuffs with a 6'1" prostitute with breasts the size of Timbuktu, and fists that had obviously seen a scrap or two before. This was NOT her first rodeo. So I just continued to ignore her, dance with my friends, and drink the pink drink. She was still hovering here and there with a look of death on her mug. Big Billy kept joking that she called her pimp to come over and rough us up since she was ranting into her flip cell phone as she paced and grazed any and all male patrons at the bar with her Mount Vesuvius bosoms.

After one, or two, or three of those gorgeous drinks, I needed to find the ladies room. Downstairs and far away from the action it was. I thought I heard heavy smashing footsteps on the stairs just a few steps behind me, but I didn't look. I went into the stall and locked the door. Then I heard the Queen of the Night starting to curse and rant in French. I turned on my phone to call Ace and tell him my life was possibly in grave danger, and I needed rescuing from the ladies room tout de suite, and to bring a posse!!!!! Unfortunately, the call was not going through. I just left that pleading message on his voicemail which he would probably receive in forty-eight hours at the expedient rate Verizon seemed to function in France.

I am not afraid of many things in this world. However, a totally intoxicated, whacked out Amazon prostitute who had it in for me, on the loose in the bowels of the Hotel Costes with nary a human in sight to prevent or even witness my murder was a little fucking scary.

She barreled into the ladies room screaming obscenities in French. I could hear her six inch hooker heels clicking on the marble floor, pacing. I was locked in my stall and literally shaking! Was she on a mission to take down an innocent American tourist tonight? Had she mistaken me for the wife of a Colombian druglord and wanted cartel revenge? Was she just coked and smoked and drunk out of her mind and strictly wanted to toy with me? Why was this happening to little, innocent me? Of all the women in the entire hotel, this psychopath chose *me* to unleash her lifetime of rage, hate and vengeance against all flat chested American women it seemed.

Whatever her motivation was, was now not my main concern. She and her six inch prostitute heels were standing right outside of my stall, we were the only two people in this vast ladies lounge. The sudden sound and sight of a long switchblade piercing though the crack in my stall door literally put me in a state of hyperventilation. Instead of the Sword of Damocles hanging over my head, the Sabre of Queen of the Night was hanging over my face and about to bring about my mortal demise.

I whispered, "What do you want?"

She laughed and laughed and said, "Oh, my little princess I just want you - cut up into small pieces. It will be a nice souvenir for my friends."

Queen of the Night started banging on my stall door while running the blade around the edges of the door. I was starting to seriously fear for my life!

Next thing I knew, there was a loud knocking at the door. Ace, Big Billy, Little Billy, Tony and a two bouncers all stormed into the loo to rescue me!

"Oh how quaint! Your little faggot American boyfriends came to protect you, well isn't that lovely!"

Now people, I am a lover, not a fighter! I have never been in a fistfight or a catfight in my life and I intend to keep it that way for the rest of my days. This Queen of the Night was not happy that whatever plan she had for me was foiled by the good ol' American tennis cavalry.

She left the hotel escorted by security and that was the end of her.

Relieved as we were (especially me), our crew stayed up drinking who-knows-how-many more pretty pink drinks - mind you this was the night before our flight the next morning, and no one knew where their tennis equipment was at this point.

We all piled into a cab and made it back to my hotel, Le Meurice on The Rivoli. I scored an amazing Presidential Suite (at a cheap Expedia price) because my friend from the New York Film Academy now lived in Paris and did P.R. for Le Meurice. The others were all staying at some three star boutique hotel near the Arc de Triomphe. In my suite I had two cases of Cabernet Franc, and two cases of Chenin Blanc from Loire. I didn't know if I was getting these on the plane or if I had to ship them from the airport.

At the ripe hour of four a.m., and with the entire crew from Hotel Costes now ensconced in my Meurice suite, I had the genius idea that we should open and sample some of the special Loire Valley wine that I had planned to bring home and give as special gifts to special people, and treasure for years to come. But hey, instead of doing that, why not decant it right here, right now with my already inebriated and surely highly appreciative posse?

Of course I travel with my Bose speaker, because I need MY amazing music available to me at all times. You seriously just cannot trust any hotel (not even a five star), to have any type of music player available beyond a clock radio. I started CRANKING Hotel Costes music (of course, to celebrate my liberation and me still being alive!), Mark Ronson, The entire Wolf of Wall Street Soundtrack, The Stones, and Big Audio Dynamite. Soon enough, the phone rang. "Hotel security, could you keep it down please? Lower the volume s'il vous plaît?"

I said, "Oui, bien sur."

I lowered the volume somewhat, but clearly *not* enough. Five minutes later security was knocking at the door, so I told him we were all celebrating me not being murdered at the Hotel Costes by a seven foot prostitute! I invited him in and told him to have a glass of wine with us and that we had to celebrate Paris tonight because we were returning to The States in the morning! He stayed, of course.

I left the door to my suite open and taped a sign to the elevator up/down buttons - "BIG PARTY IN ROOM 852," with stick figure illustrations of us dancing and drinking wine.

Next thing we knew, the French golf team was partying in our suite, Carla Bruni (The President was not with her this night), Emilia Clarke and her boyfriend, and I think one of Carla's bodyguards. We cranked the music louder and louder and danced until the sun came up and only one bottle of wine was left. I hid this in my suitcase as a real souvenir. I plan to drink this fine bottle of Cabernet Franc on my 100th birthday with my family and friends and I will retell this tale sparing none of the juicy details!

VIVE LA FRANCE!!!

'Twas The Night Before Thanksgiving

'Twas the night before Thanksgiving, when all through the hotel
Not a creature was stirring, not even a man with a bell;
The swimsuits were hung in the gift shop with care,
In hopes that new guests with credit cards soon would be there.

The tourists were nestled all snug in strange beds
While visions of sunshine and tryptophan danced in their heads;
Sitting in the lobby, wine in my mitt,
Ecstatic my stalker was absent, not being a twit.

When out by the pool there arose such a crash
Alas, just an errant frat boy inciting a beer bottle smash;
I walked to the terrace to take a small peek,
And saw it was more than just one collegiate geek.

The moon on the golf course outshone by fake lights
Gave the luster of a carnival to an otherwise ethereal sight;
When what to my sleep deprived eyes should appear,
A South American polo player sitting quite near.

With a dark tan, dark hair, slick and macho
I knew in a moment it must be St. Nacho;
More gorgeous than a Greek god in white jeans so stunning,
He snapped a finger, and twenty-two models came running.

Now Giselle! Now Karlie! Now Catherine and Natalia!
Or, Jessica! Or, Lara! Or Coco! Or Tanya!
To the edge of the bar! To the side of the pool!
Doesn't matter who sits on Nacho's lap he always looks cool!

As spectators that before an orator spy
A crowd was growing and I didn't know why;
So up to the penthouse the models they strode,
On stilettos with Nacho to the top of the abode.

And then in a second, I heard a strange sound
"Mummy, mummy", so I instantly turned around;
A tiny tot so foreign and pert,
I could tell by his lederhosen he was from Frankfurt.

He was dressed all in velvet from his hair to his toes
He just hopped off a plane and didn't change clothes;
He was staring at the pool, yearning for a dip,
But it was after midnight, and he was spent from his trip.

He then wandered off to his mummy and daddy
When out of the corner of my eye, I saw Rory's caddy;
I knew him from many a PGA tourney,
He stopped for a drink after the 18 hole journey.

By this hour the pool had evolved into a club scene
Gorgeous girls and guys all in need of visine;
Instead of snow, ice and turkeys up in the north,
I was surrounded by beautiful people which propelled me forth.

There in the twinkling moonlight I spied
A slunk over drunk model who had surely just cried;

Her mascara was smeared, halter hanging on loosely
I helped her off the ground and she thanked me profusely.

She asked if I was here to forget about snow
Said her friends from Dartmouth had mountains of blow;
Reunited with a fresh drink and with her best friend,
She clearly did not want the evening to end.

Such is the state of affairs down here at the beach
I would be writing a masterpiece but my laptop's out of reach;
I wish you the most excellent of Thanksgivings,
I hope you get to eat/relax/watch the parade with no misgivings!

Running Away From Home Across the Street

Eighth grade was a big year for me; I was turning thirteen and only yearned for one thing – a phone in my room. Some of my friends had phones in their rooms and believe it or not, this was a *big* deal, and so I *had* to have one too. I was looking forward to lying on my preppy pink Laura Ashley comforter, and having leisurely chats, sharing gossip and calling boys from the privacy of my own room, rather than the status quo of stretching the cord across the kitchen floor and sequestering myself on the pantry floor to have a private conversation.

My birthday is in September, so I had been working on my mom all summer. "When I get my own phone, I won't be gabbing in the kitchen all the time anymore and be in your way," or, "When I get my own phone I will get my homework done faster because I can sit at my desk and talk to the smartest kid in math." "I'll probably be smarter because having my own phone will make me just stay in my room and study more." I had an endless spiel of ridiculous reasons why it was a good thing for my mom to let me have my own phone. By the end of August, I think she just acquiesced and said yes to stop me from nagging her to death.

Should I get the pink princess design to match my room? The sleek one piece black design from Sharper Image? It would be really cool to have the Bang and Olufsen uber modern design like my friend Kimmie's father had in his office, but my mom would never spend that much on a kid's phone.

I told all my friends I was getting a phone in my room for my birthday. "Ooh, luck-ee", and "That is so rad." I planned to show it off at my slumber party the Friday after my actual birthday.

On the morning of September 19th, I awoke to no phone in my room (I guess I thought the elves would magically install it in the night). So I just figured I would get it later with all my presents at dinner. After dinner at my favorite steakhouse, I opened my presents, but NO phone! I asked my parents, "Oh, is my phone being installed tomorrow?" My dad looked at me and said, "Your grades really aren't where we want them to be right now, so we decided if you get a 3.5 or higher on your next report card, you may have the phone." "It is a privilege to have a phone in your room and blah, blah, blah…"

WHAT???? Where did they get this stuff? Was my mom reading those idiotic self-help books again? A few titles I saw floating through the house were "How to Survive Your Teenager," "Raising a Healthy and Happy Teen," and the killer was "Taking Control; Your Teen *Wants* Discipline." I didn't know about the *rest* of America, but *I* sure as hell didn't want discipline, and neither did any other teens I knew. Whenever I saw this propaganda around my house, I would wrap it in paper towels and throw it straight into the garbage! How dare my parents read this junk and try and "outsmart" me? If my mom asked, "Did you see such and such book around?" I would just give her a blank stare.

I felt like they just didn't want me to have my own phone and the grade speech was just an excuse. How annoying and archaic could my parents be? Why couldn't I have cool parents? How dangerous could it be for me to have my own phone? Would I be calling secret agents? Older boys? Having phone sex? What's the big deal? I tried to reason, beg and plead with them for at least another hour that night, but it got me nowhere. I went to bed totally perturbed and vowing to get my phone somehow.

The next morning on the bus, I told my BFF Ann that I did *not* get my phone, but that I had a surefire plan to make it happen. I would run away from home, move in with Ann and tell my parents I'm not coming home until the phone is installed. Brilliant!

That day after school, I informed my mom that I would be moving out until my phone was in my room. The news somehow didn't garner the reaction I had hoped for.

She barely looked up from her paper to say, "That's nice dear."

I expected her to try and stop her precious daughter from running away from home, but she didn't seem that concerned. Clearly this was not her first rodeo.

Ann and I carried two dressers and their contents across the street, virtually all the hanging clothes in my closets, my stereo system, soccer trophies, my Cure and Big Audio Dynamite posters, and Smiths *Meat is Murder* poster.

I was making a statement. No matter what, I was dead serious about moving out until I got my phone. I even brought my onion bagels, Schweppes ginger ale, and Pepperidge Farm chocolate chip cookie stash in case Ann's mom tried to make me eat their weird Southern food. I recall my mom waving goodbye with a sly grin on her face as we carried the last load through the foyer and out the front door.

As soon as I settled into my new digs across the street, I knew life was about to be very different for me. Mrs. Lombardo gave me a lecture before I even finished taping my last Cure poster to Ann's wall.

"Honey, you are welcome to stay as long as you like, but you must follow *my* rules. Bedtime and lights out at nine, setting the table and doing the dishes, and any other chores my kids do," she informed with a satisfied smile.

Five minutes in Chez Lombardo and I was already missing home. Bedtime at nine? What is she, insane? I haven't had lights out at nine since third grade. My escape house was looking more and more like basic training at Fort Bragg. She brought Ann and me a few baskets of clean towels and instructed us to "fold". I never had to do this stuff on demand at my house. But I was on a mission to get my phone, and a few chores would not stop me.

The Lombardo family was from Tennessee, and the denizens of my neighborhood just didn't know what to make of their quirky Southern ways. In the hood, most of the dads worked, mowed the lawn, and the moms did mom stuff while the kids played soccer in the backyard. Typical suburban life.

Life was really different at the Lombardo homestead. For starters, the "Rebel" flag was floating in the wind on their flagpole; it was also displayed proudly in the garage, and the family room I believe. They had two dogs (one was named Bubba!), three cats, a few birds and God knows what other creatures. The kids said "Yes, sir," and "Yes ma'am," when addressing their parents and other grown-ups, and actually listened to their parents! The kid's rooms were decorated with Elvis posters – WTF? Elvis? I guess they hadn't discovered Depeche Mode or Sigue Sigue Sputnik in Tennessee yet.

In the summer, the mom (a knockout) would mow the lawn in a string bikini. In the winter, you could find the dad getting the mail in his robe while smoking a cigar and traipsing through the snow in his bare feet. They had two boys and two girls, and they were all good looking, fun kids. Pretty soon, all the boys on the block and at school were crazy for Ann, who was very pretty and the sweet Southern accent didn't hurt. They were a definite spark of much needed energy and eccentricity to our neighborhood. My dad thought it was just ducky to see the Mrs. mowing the lawn, especially in a bikini.

The first few days of my fugitive lifestyle went well. Ann and I did everything together anyway, except now I just slept over. I was never a huge believer of studying, or doing too much schoolwork unless it was absolutely necessary. I usually did just the bare minimum and still managed at least a 3.0, so I figured - why miss out on all the fun things in life to do homework? After all, I was planning on doing something *artsy*, not *mathy* or *sciencey*. Anyway, I had a routine for things I absolutely *loathed,* like science. I was mostly a jock, but I was friends with all the brainy kids in class too, even the smartest kid in science, Doug. He was pretty cool for being such a nerd. So if I didn't study, I would just feign illness, go into school late (or not at all), miss the test, and take it the following day. I think I paid him twenty dollars per test and he would write down the answers, which I would smuggle into class either written cryptically on my folder, or taped to my thighs under my skirt, and just lift it up for the answers during the make-up test.

On the third morning of my self-imposed exile, the alarm clock rang at the usual hour of six something. Ann tried to get me up, but I told her I didn't study for the science exam and I was planning on going in after the third period. She didn't say anything, and I went back to sleep. I was having a dream about Macbeth because my term paper was due at the end of the week. In my dream I envisioned a horrifying, monstrous figure looming above me, at first I thought it was Banquo's ghost, then I rubbed my eyes and saw something far scarier.

This vision was about as welcome to me as Banquo's ghost was to Macbeth. A wild eyed lunatic was menacing above me like a nightmare, except it was real.

I said, "Oh, Mrs. Lombardo, I didn't study for my science test, so I can't go in 'til the third period, can you give me a ride to school around ten?"

This simple question enraged the beast even further. Mrs. Lombardo was glaring at me with fierce, glowing, and I swear, *red* eyeballs bulging out of her head. She had somehow morphed into Rambo (another Lombardo icon, the poster displayed right next to Elvis). She screamed louder than an army sergeant, "GET OUT OF BED GIRL!!!", "I don't know what goes on at your house, but we do NOT skip school here!" "Get your behind on that bus NOW!"

I looked up and said something like, "Oh, this is *not* working for me. I think I have to move out now. I'll get the rest of my stuff later."

Mrs. Lombardo was *not* happy. Maybe she took me in to try to reform my slacker ways, or try to teach me how to be an obedient child, but whatever the reason, I don't think she envisioned this particular outcome. She looked at me like, "Well, I tried!", and rolled her eyes.

Within a few days of moving back home, I got the phone. I don't remember what exactly I said to finally convince the rents (as we endearingly referred to them), but I guess they realized it meant quite a lot to me and they caved. They were creating a monster by always giving me what I wanted, but I wasn't about to tell *them* that. They should have figured it out on their own from reading one of their self-help teenager books!

Pine Forest

Now that Christmas is over, I am reflecting on Christmases past as I put away all of the decorations at my house.

When I grew up, we always had a live Christmas tree which was just the norm. I was the youngest of five children, so by the time I was in eighth grade my mom had somehow lost her enthusiasm for Christmas. I came home from school one day, and there, sitting in the family room was a *fake* Christmas tree! I immediately ran through the house screaming "Mom, mom, MOM," at the top of my lungs like a lunatic.

My mother was on the phone upstairs and looked at me like, "What's the big emergency?"

I said, "How could you get a fake, plastic, horrible tree for our house for Christmas!?" I started crying and said, "You ruined my Christmas! I will not live in a house with a fake Christmas tree, I will move out first," (yes, I was very dramatic). I told her I would buy a real and beautiful tree with my own money from my allowance.

My mother said, "Real Christmas trees are a bother, they need to be watered daily, the needles are everywhere and it's such a mess. This tree looks real (only if you are on Quaaludes!) with no fuss at all."

I cried, "M-O-M are you crazy? You just don't GET IT! Christmas is about the REAL tree, the smell, the falling needles and the mess too! It's about the cutout sugar cookies that take us two days to finish, playing Christmas music, wrapping presents together, going to church on Christmas

Eve, and then watching the black and white version of Scrooge! Those are the things that make it Christmas. Are we going to have fake Christmas cookies this year too mom?"

She thought I was a little nuts for getting this worked up over a tree, but she was actively
ignoring my rant at this point and said the discussion was "closed." I knew my mom well enough to realize I either had to get my dad to buy a tree when he came home, or do it myself.

I grew up in a great neighborhood called Collingwood in upstate New York. The reason it was so great was because tons of fun, cool kids lived there, and we all did the usual things kids and teenagers do. Ride bikes, play spin the bottle, sneak liquor from our parents when we were older, etc. We had a "gang" consisting of all the hip kids, (no brainy dorks allowed please) which was about half guys and half girls. We were all platonic friends for the most part, and it was quite the motley crew.

To add to our crew, a new family from Newcastle, England moved on the block. They had three kids , (Thank God!), and introduced us provincial pipsqueaks to some new, wicked stuff from across the pond. The Psychedelic Furs, Thomas Dolby, down duvets for your bed (we all had scratchy Sears comforters), zed rather than z, al-YOU-min-ium foil, and saying AH-dee-daz, instead of a-DEE-diss for the brand Adidas.

There was one boy who was older than me, Simon, and two little sisters (whatever). In no time flat, Simon was head over heels in love with me, and hanging around my house all the time like a puppy dog. Kind of sickening – doing my math and science homework for me, asking my mom if she needed help bringing in groceries, or clearing up the dirty dishes in the kitchen. What a kiss ass. My dad was usually never home, so my mom thought Simon was *charming.*

"What a nice boy," and "English children have the best manners," she would say.

UGH. I tolerated Simon at our house because he was totally abusable. I could mock his thick Newcastle accent, make him eat weird recipes I was trying out, and take his family crest ring hostage; which I pretended went down the garbage disposal and into pureed history. After an hour of his arm down the kitchen sink, I produced the ring on a silver tray, and had the best laugh of my life! It seemed the more I tortured Simon, the more he loved me.

Now, getting back to the tree. After my mom ignored my screaming, crying and stalking her about the fake Christmas tree that day, I had an idea. Just like the Grinch---a wonderful, awful idea!

I picked up the phone with a cord attached to the actual phone, and pressed the buttons, (yes, it was *after* dial phones) and dialed Simon's number. 745-7199, I still remember it.

"Ellooooo," his mum said.

"Is Simon there please?" Which is how we asked for people on the phone in the 80's.

"Elloow," said Simon.

"Hi Simon, it's me---I need you to come over and help me with a project."

Simon said, "Okaaayy then, I'll be right oveeeuerr," in his strong Newcastle brogue.

He lived down the next street seven houses away, so I knew I had about ten minutes until he walked over and rang the doorbell. My father was not much of a handyman, but he had a very organized garage with every tool imaginable. So, I found an axe, a saw, a flashlight (or as Simon said, electric torch), and anything else I thought might come in handy for chopping down a tree. I stuffed it all into the biggest duffel bag I could find, and dragged it to the front door, ready to go.

Simon arrived and said, "So, what's this project then?"

"Well, Simon, remember when you said you would do ANYTHING for me?"

Simon, "Ummmm yes."

"Well the deal is my mom bought a fake, horrible Christmas tree, and I just won't let this happen. We are going to Pine Forest to chop down the best tree we can find, bring it back, and put it in my family room!" I said.

Simon said "Ok," and didn't question my plan.

That was good since I didn't actually have a plan other than walking the roughly two miles into the woods in the dark, freezing cold, dead of winter to procure the world's most perfect pine tree. I think he thought I was crazy too, but he didn't say anything.

Simon knew the way to Pine Forest. He was two years older than me, and his friends, Bryan, Eric, Mark, and Chris all lived in the hood and found Pine Forest first before any of the girls knew about it. It was just a fun hike from our street in the summer, and nothing ever really happened in Pine Forest except we all split a bottle of wine and played spin the bottle once. No one ever went there in the winter.

Simon and I made it to the heart of Pine Forest, where I saw a glorious ten foot blue spruce.

"That's the one!" I exclaimed.

I handed him the axe and told him to hack it down. It was getting colder and colder, and the snow was falling steadily. The axe from my house was either too small or too dull, in any case, after a good ten minutes (a long time in the dark, snowy forest) we weren't making progress.

Simon said, "This tree is too big, the trunk is too thick, and the axe is too dull!"

Not to be persuaded from my dream tree, I grabbed the axe and said, "Forget it, I will do it!"

The axe *was* dull, and I didn't know what the hell I was doing. I tried the saw next, but that seemed as if it would take a century to cut through the trunk, or else I would lose a finger first. The flimsy saw, which was probably a $20 Joe-homeowner-saw from Sears, simply was not cutting the mustard – or the tree. I realized we just didn't have the proper tools, and it was getting colder.

Simon suggested a slightly smaller, sparser tree, maybe seven or eight feet tall, with a skinnier apron of branches. At this point it looked good to me since it had a reasonable looking size trunk I thought he had a chance at cleaving through, and it wasn't plastic. He chopped away at the tree, making good progress, with me cheering him on.

"Come on Simon! You can do it! Almost done – let's go!"

Finally the tree was down! Simon dragged the tree back to my house, while I hoisted the duffle bag with the hacking instruments. We were both frozen and exhausted when we got back to my house.

The first thing I did was lug the fake, horrible, vile, non-biodegradable piece of crap to the living room. I instructed Simon to put the new tree in the pride of place spot at the end of the family room. I made Simon and I some hot chocolate and I decorated the entire tree myself in one hour flat.

I made myself in charge of buying the Christmas tree every year henceforth. I would tell my mom, "Don't worry, dad and I are getting the tree."

After the whole Pine Forest ordeal, my mother never interfered with my tree decorating endeavors again. The new regime was: the fake tree was put up in the living room every year with boring white lights and pink ribbons (yes it was the 80's), and kind of became my mom's tree. The real tree was always in the traditional spot in the family room decorated with colored lights and all of the family decorations from over the years.

As for my adult Christmas tree experiences, I always had a little but real tree from the corner deli in my New York apartment. When I moved into a house I always bought a real tree, the biggest I could find, but my dog Bowie started peeing on it in his old age, he must have been delusional and thought it was a tree outside. I am ashamed to admit I actually bought a fake tree. The fake tree was a mammoth and very expensive and real looking piece of plastic, but that didn't take away the *plastic factor*. I am proud to say I recycled it with all of the Christmas trash this year. I am now headed back to the land of real Christmas trees!

So – who wants to go to Pine Forest?

I Left My Teeth in Sarasota

I was seeing this guy quite a bit older than me and he invited me to go to Sarasota to visit his ninety-seven year old stepmother. Now Sarasota is not my cup of tea, but I figured - it's forty degrees warmer in Sarasota than it is in New York, so why not go?

After landing on a gorgeous, sunny day, then being stuck in gridlock traffic for over an hour, I realized it's true. Everyone over the age of seventy leaves the northeast and lives in Florida *and* drives a Buick aimlessly for the rest of their natural born lives.

I really wanted to stay in a hotel, especially since my boyfriend had promised me the last *three* visits to the old folks home we wouldn't have to stay there again. Alas, back to the youth center we returned.

Upon entering the building, one is greeted with the pungent scent of senior citizens, no malice intended, but there is a certain not-so-fresh odor wafting through the air at all times. The empty living room lobby connotes a feeling of gloom as there is nary a soul in sight. One wonders, are the oldsters all napping in their single beds? Are they having a quick game of bingo in the dining room before their dinner? Are they out scoring come choice blow since they only have a few years or weeks left? Hopefully they were all out doing something fun, maybe spending their family's future inheritance like drunken sailors at Van Cleef & Arpels or at the track.

The first two dates of our visit, boyfriend and I spent the days out and about looking for some culture, coffee, liveliness, and some form of life without a walker. Then we picked up the step-mother and went off into the great frontier for dinner.

The first night we dined at Botticelli, which is basically a trumped up goomba Tony Soprano-esque dated dining establishment with mauve chairs which sank two feet into the ground as we were seated. As the frigid air (even though it was a gorgeous ninety degree evening outdoors) enveloped my body, I clutched the vinyl faux crocodile menu for life and tried to peek above table level. The scent of very old, very putrid Chanel number 5 filled my nostrils from the woman at the table next to us.

The dinner clientele was a mix of older couples, and much older men with younger busty dates in faux Louboutins. The entrees were mostly stand by continental fare at inflated prices while an off key piano dinged 70's music in the bar. After visiting the ladies room with two plugged up toilets, I took this restaurant off my places to visit in the future.

The second evening of our visit, we dined at a surprisingly delightful and delicious French restaurant, Mason Blanche. In contrast to the previous evening's dining experience everything about this French restaurant was pleasant. The maitre'd took care to lead us to our table and seat us thoughtfully. The chairs were hip, modern round leather surrounding a table of linen which was crisp and spotless, the flatware and china were modern, sleek and euro. The scent of succulent white lilies from our table filled my nostrils and my mind with happy French thoughts. This place had a somewhat younger, hipper vibe than the previous evening of quasi cadaver diners. They were even playing some very hip French music by MC Solaar, which lifted my spirits immeasurably. This quaint little spot was a dose of culture and a true culinary delight. This gave me some sense of relief for the hopefully never to happen day that I myself would wind up living in an old age neighborhood.

The next evening, we were informed by the step-mother that we were going to be enjoying the samplings of the old folks home restaurant. I was just going to wear a pair of jeans, a white blouse, and some flats, and eschew hair and make-up except for a ponytail and some pink lip gloss.

At the last minute I decided I didn't have to sport something dreary and boring akin to the Belk wearing Florida denizens. Instead I would wear what I really wanted to wear - and dazzle the former jet set. I donned my new spiffy Prada loafers, Prada houndstooth pants (from three seasons ago, but how would this group know the difference), and a cute Kate Spade top with heavily a rhinestoned Peter Pan collar that was very Audrey Hepburn. I sprayed some dry shampoo in my hair and flooffed it way out, I lined my eyes with eyeliner, put on mascara, a light dusting of pressed Dior powder and some major Hollywood bright red lipstick.

As we entered the dining room with the step-mother, all heads turned to stare. Not only was step-mom's senior standing raised an ante by having family visit her, but it was taken to the next notch since I was looking so fashionable. One lady stood up and stopped me on the way to our table and commented on my outfit.

"You look so stunning, I love color, and you just made my day," she said.

After we were seated and the waiter came over and asked us if we wanted drinks, I said, "Ten shots of tequila please!"

He laughed and thought I was serious, and probably couldn't wait to see some people actually having fun while at his job. I asked him if he offers free cocktails to all the residents just for the fun of it. If I worked there I would give them all tons of free liquor and watch the antics begin!

Boyfriend wasn't talking during dinner, step-mom wasn't talking, and anyone who knows me knows that I am a very animated dinner companion. I decided it was up to *me* to start a conversation at our table, and try to lighten the mood a little bit by making these two stiffies laugh.

"Alice," I said, "so tell me the dirt on this place - who is the casa nova here and who is the village floozy?"

"Oh, I don't follow that nonsense and I don't care," was her reply.

Boring answer. I mean if one lives in an old folks home - the highlight of your day would be the local gossip which must be salacious and really, what else is there to do other than booze it up and cause some havoc?

I said, "Look at all these single, lonely diners. Do they have a matchmaking service here that connects two lonely hearts and gives them the opportunity to have dinner with a new friend and share a meal and some time together? I would rather eat with a nice man than eat alone, or eat with girl-friends and have some conversation and fun."

Alice said, "Well there is a table where single diners can all eat together."

I asked, "Well, why don't you sit there instead of by yourself most of the time?"

Alice sighed, "The people at the table are all crazy, and so annoying you would rather skip the meal entirely than dine with that group of misfits!"

I pointed out a handsome, male, lonely, single diner at a table nearby, and a nice looking lady alone at the table next to him . I said, "If I worked here, I would get those two together and hope for the best! "

Alice looked at the man and said, "Oh *him*, he is from England and he is a real *pill*. I have said good morning and good evening to him for the past ten years and he doesn't even answer! He's so rude!"

Boyfriend and I drank our martinis (we skipped the wine as it was all five dollars a glass) as quickly as possible and tried to enjoy the culinary servings. It wasn't easy, but we were starving, and as they say, hunger is the best appetizer.

A few minutes later, the Englishman walked by our table.

"Toodleoo." I said, not expecting him to answer.

Well, didn't Mr. Englishman get a twinkle in his eye and say, "Hello there!" Then he started to chat me up.

I was shocked he answered and said, " I heard you are English and I *love* England."

He said, "No, actually I am from Scotland."

I said, "OH! I LOVE Scotland! I went to Glamis Castle, Holyroodhouse, Edinburgh Castle, Balmoral, I love the

Queen Mother, I love Edinburgh, Glasgow, and everything about Scotland!"

I told him I would love to live there even though it is cold and gloomy most of the time. I told him my favorite place of all time in the United Kingdom is Gleneagles and that there is just something magical about Scotland.

Well, he was thrilled to bits and couldn't have been nicer. He introduced himself and gave me his card which was embellished with his family tartan of course. Viscount Trevor Campbell.

A titled member of the peerage living in an upscale old folks home in (gulp) Florida? "That just ain't right," I thought.

"Why did you leave your land and your home in Scotland?" I asked.

"It's a long story. My evil kids made me come here. They both live in the states. It is easier for them to park me here then it is for them to have me on the loose at Ben Nevis Castle spending money on hunting parties and wine. They tell me I'm here for my health but that's a crock! I miss Scotland everyday, and I'm glad to find someone around this Godforsaken place who feels the same. You have an open invitation to Ben Nevis Castle as long as I'm still kicking, and I know for sure you would brighten up the place!"

"Thanks a million!" I answered. I wanted to cry for Trevor. How lonely he looked and getting kicked out of the castle, even if it wasn't for the whole year, was simply unfair. I would be packed in two seconds to be Trevor's court jester, his reader of classic books, or the amateur sommelier for this cool ninety something year old viscount.

When he turned to leave, I looked at step-mom who was bowled over with shock. I didn't want her feelings to be hurt since, after all these years, he said hello to me but never to her.

I said, "Well, he's a nice enough fellow, but I think I"m too old for him!"

What a laugh we had! For reference, when dining at a retirement center, it is always better to sip your martini and tell a joke than to just sit there and soak in the potentially depressing atmosphere.

After dinner, the highlight of the evening was to go into the catacombs - I mean the auditorium - for a performance of a piano prodigy who had been entertaining residents at the old folks home for years. We found a spot for three somewhere in the last few rows. The piano player had a face made of plastic, I think he was male, and probably twenty-five, but looked like he was twelve and sounded like a little girl. He announced in a soft whisper, " I am now going to play you a ba-LAWD from Mozart. Was he saying ballad? He said it that way more than once, so I was trying desperately not to laugh my head off.

I looked at boyfriend and he was pointing out that the man in front of us was fast asleep, and snoring loudly, while his wife was jerking his suit jacket and trying to wake him up. I looked around the room and noticed that about eighty percent of the audience was asleep. This was really too much to bear! Next, boyfriend started pushing his foot towards the rear end of the sleeping man in front of us, pretending he was going to kick him. We both started giggling uncontrollably, and Alice was not too pleased with us.

I took two bathroom breaks and got up for water a few times just to get through the unbearable ten or so pieces this guy was playing. He really was a beautiful and talented piano player, it was just the tomblike atmosphere with no alcohol that really killed the vibe.

After the performance, boyfriend and I looked at each other in *huge* relief, and we all made it to the lobby. While waiting for the elevator, I noticed a white napkin on the floor with something sticking out under the call button. I thought I must have been hallucinating.

I gasped in horror and looked and looked until I realized what I was seeing! A set of false teeth in the napkin!

I grabbed boyfriend's arm and said, "Look, look, look! Someone left their teeth on the floor!"

He couldn't believe his eyes either and said, "Alice! What is that?"

Alice was not fazed at all and replied, "I don't know."

Boyfriend exclaimed, "Someone left their teeth on the floor!"

Alice chuckled, "I have *never* seen that before!"

A *perfect* ending to a fantastic evening.

The Sophia Questionnaire

1. How old were you when you lost your virginity?
2. Were you in love?
3. What is your favorite song?
4. What is your favorite band?
5. Are you a member of the mile high club?
6. What is the strangest place you have ever made love?
7. What is your favorite novel?
8. If you could take the day off tomorrow, what would you do?
9. If you could take an entire month off, where would you go?
10. What is your favorite meal?
11. What is your favorite city?
12. What is your favorite age?
13. What is your pet cause?
14. What is your pet peeve?
15. What is your favorite vacation spot?
16. What is your favorite feature film?
17. What is your favorite piece of classical music?
18. What is your favorite breed of dog?
19. What is your favorite body of water?
20. What is your favorite pizza topping?
21. Men - Boxers or briefs?
22. Women- flats or heels?

23. What is your favorite hotel in the U.S.?
24. What is your favorite hotel in the world?
25. What was the first car you ever owned?
26. What is the car you currently drive?
27. What was your first job, and how much did you earn per hour?
28. What is the favorite job that you have ever had?
29. What is your favorite sport to play?
30. What is your favorite sport to watch?
31. Who was your favorite relative when you were growing up?
32. What is your favorite work of art?
33. Who is your favorite artist?
34. What is your favorite museum?
35. What is the best rock concert you have ever attended?
36. Power muff, landing strip or Brazilian?
37. La Perla or Agent Provocateur?
38. If you could be a character in any movie, who would you want to be?
39. How many cases of wine have you consumed in your lifetime (an estimate)?

I developed *The Sophia Questionnaire* because I grew tired of reading the Proust Questionnaire which is used in *Vanity Fair* to interview public figures. Proust made this quiz popular, hence the name. However, I feel it is obtuse, obsolete, and not truly indicative of anyone's personality, not to mention it completely lacks any fun whatsoever.

I want *Vanity Fair* to publish my *fun* version, and then *The Sophia Questionnaire* will be in the back of the magazine!

Look for my answers to this questionnaire on my upcoming website www.swingingfromthechandeliers.com Or read the answers in my next book of short stories.

Made in the USA
Columbia, SC
02 April 2022